THE FOURTH DIMENSION
OF FOREIGN POLICY:
EDUCATIONAL AND CULTURAL
AFFAIRS

THE FOURTH DIMENSION
OF FOREIGN POLICY:
EDUCATIONAL
AND CULTURAL AFFAIRS

by PHILIP H. COOMBS

Published for the
Council on Foreign Relations
by
Harper & Row, Publishers
New York and Evanston

The Council on Foreign Relations is a non-profit institution devoted to study of the international aspects of American political, economic and strategic problems. It takes no stand, expressed or implied, on American policy.

The authors of books published under the auspices of the Council are responsible for their statements of fact and expressions of opinion. The Council is responsible only for determining that they should be presented to the public.

IN MEMORY OF EDWARD JOHN NOBLE

The Policy Book series of the Council on Foreign Relations is published under a grant from the Edward John Noble Foundation in memory of Mr. Noble and his interest in encouraging American leadership.

Policy Books of the Council on Foreign Relations

This volume is one of a series of short books on important subjects related to United States foreign policy. The purpose of these Policy Books is twofold: first, to provide readers in this country and elsewhere with essays and analytical studies of the highest quality of problems of world significance; second, to contribute to constructive thinking on American policies for the future. These books make a virtue of brevity, not with the aim of oversimplification, but to present with a minimum of factual background and detail the reasoned conclusions of individual authors with first-hand experience and special qualifications.

The Council was fortunate in persuading Philip Coombs to write this book. As Assistant Secretary of State, Mr. Coombs had much to do with the greater emphasis that is now placed on education and cultural relations as a vital component of foreign policy. That experience, as well as his lifetime of concern with the subject, lends great weight to the views he expresses here. The Council is greatly indebted to the Carnegie Corporation of New York for its financial support to Mr. Coombs while he was writing his book.

The Council and the author wish to express their deep appreciation to Senator J. W. Fulbright for the Foreword which he has contributed.

While the manuscript was in preparation and before it reached final form, the author had the benefit of the advice and comments of an expert group invited to discuss it at two meetings. The Council wishes to thank the following participants: John W.

Gardner (Chairman), James P. Baxter, 3rd, Robert Blum, William A. M. Burden, Frederick Burkhardt, Donald B. Cook, W. Phillips Davison, John S. Fischer, Donald Henderson, John B. Howard, Waldemar Nielsen, Herbert Passin, George N. Shuster, Albert G. Sims and Carleton Sprague Smith.

Responsibility for the statements of fact and opinion rests with the author, not with the group, the Council, or the Carnegie Corporation. The Council takes responsibility for the decision to publish the book as a contribution to thought on a subject of real though often inadequately recognized significance, one that relates foreign policy to the people who are its reason for being and gives substance to alliances, foreign aid, and the search for peace.

JOHN C. CAMPBELL
Editor

Foreword

By Senator J. W. Fulbright

Foreign policy cannot be based on military posture and diplomatic activities alone in today's world. The shape of the world a generation from now will be influenced far more by how well we communicate the values of our society to others than by our military or diplomatic superiority. The question of whether the highest aspirations of mankind can best be fulfilled under a totalitarian or a democratic society will ultimately be decided in the minds of men—not on a battlefield or in a conference room. In viewing the challenge in this manner, the importance of the human element in foreign policy becomes quite obvious. The fundamental requirement for a world community of good neighbors is that all different peoples achieve a broader and deeper mutual understanding of each other. Such an understanding can be promoted through people-to-people contacts outside formal diplomatic channels. We may not be able to buy friends even if we tried—and our policies have at times invited such criticism—but we can *win* them through programs which allow foreigners to get to know us and us to know them. These mutual exposures to foreign peoples and cultures leave little doubt about the existence of a "community of mankind."

Since World War II the United States has strengthened the political, military, and economic dimensions of its foreign policy. In the process we have not emphasized sufficiently the significance of the basic human factors from which a peaceful world must ultimately be built. By neglecting the human side of foreign policy we have failed to exploit adequately the fundamental strengths of our own free society—our creative scholars, artists, and writers, and our educational, research and cultural institutions.

In the decades to come international relations will be profoundly affected by the success or failure of education, as used in its broad sense, in breaking through the barriers of ignorance and distrust which divide nations and peoples, and so often set them against each other. The world has become united in the purely physical sense of economic and technological interdependence, while in psychological terms the world remains divided into mutually suspicious national communities which value their separate sovereignty over their common humanity. The purpose of international education, indeed of all education, is to help close the dangerous gap between the economic and technological interdependence of the peoples of the world and the misconceptions and myths which keep them apart. Education is in reality one of the basic factors of international relations—quite as important as diplomacy and military power in its implications for war or peace.

There are, of course, limitations on what can be accomplished by international education. The proper and realistic task of education is to help temper the excesses of emotional nationalism and to create in their stead bonds of sympathy and understanding among nations. Our long-term objective must be the development of a sense of community in the world, a feeling of shared values and interest, a feeling that effective communication is possible, and a feeling of trust and confidence in each other's purposes. In time we may even hope that the dogmatism and fanaticism which now separate the Communist nations from the free nations will gradually give way to a more enlightened and civilized view of the world paving the way for a more cooperative community of mankind.

Only since World War II ended American isolation has the United States sought to develop intensive cultural and educational relations with the rest of the world. We and the other peoples of the world have come a long way in getting to know each other since then, but we have scarcely approached the universally espoused goal of "mutual understanding." Our educational exchange program has been rewarding and we can take pride in some of the accomplishments under it, but the world has changed greatly since passage of the Educational Exchange Act of 1946.

An educational exchange program adequate to the world of 1946 is not adequate for the realities of international relations today. The Mutual Educational and Cultural Exchange Act passed by the Congress in 1961 updated our basic exchange authority, but we have failed to establish a proper role for the human side of foreign relations. Educational exchange is not merely a laudable experiment, but a *positive* instrument of foreign policy, designed to mobilize human resources just as military and economic policies seek to mobilize physical resources.

The 1961 Act which consolidated and expanded the educational exchange programs of the United States represented a partial accommodation to the realities of the 1960s, but a partial accommodation is not enough. Our educational exchange efforts over the past decade have fallen steadily behind expanding world needs, particularly with respect to Africa and Latin America. Despite the fact that the number of countries participating in the exchange programs conducted by the Department of State has doubled over the last ten years, the number of exchangees, leaders, specialists, scholars, and teachers has increased by less than 30 per cent in the same period. The total cost of all international cultural programs sponsored by the United States government adds up to less than 1 per cent of our total military budget. Our massive defense expenditures are an unfortunate necessity, but they will avail us little if we fail to make an adequate effort in the field of ideas and human understanding.

The intellectual hunger in the world today is as widespread and intense as the desire for a better material life and, indeed, the two aspirations are closely related. Especially in the nations of Asia, Africa, and Latin America the craving and need for knowledge and understanding have grown rapidly as these have been recognized as essential ingredients of a better life. We have come far in recognizing the intimate relationship between our own national interests and the economic objectives of the underdeveloped countries. Our interests are equally related to the realization of their intellectual and spiritual aspirations.

It is the task of education to break through the myths and misconceptions which feed upon ignorance. Education must lead us to a full awareness of the limitations, as well as the possibilities of human effort. If we are to survive the tide of social revolution that troubles the world and to help guide it toward a more civilized order, we must approach the upheavals of our time with a greater understanding of their diversity and complexity and with an equally clear understanding of the limitations of our own power and wisdom. If there is any lesson to be learned from history it is that the doctrines and the causes that arouse men to passion and violence are transitory; that more often than not they fade into irrelevance with the erosion of time and circumstance. We must learn to conduct international relations with patience, tolerance, openness of mind, and, most of all, with a sense of history. These are the qualities of educated men. They are the qualities we and all peoples of all races and creeds must aspire to, and make progress toward achieving, if mankind is to flourish on this earth.

We have the basic authority and the capabilities to forge a strong foreign policy tool of people-to-people communication. What is needed most to improve international understanding is greater *domestic* understanding—by the public, Congress and the Executive Branch—of the unique and fundamental importance of the human factors in international affairs. The over-all success of our very limited exchange program is unquestioned even by those who have been critical of some aspects of it. Unfortunately, it has never been given an opportunity to succeed on a larger, more realistic scale.

Small as it has been, the program has created a new climate of hope for the people-to-people approach to foreign affairs. The concluding words of the recent report to Congress by the President's Advisory Committee emphasized the possibilities this way: "In a time when most international activities seem almost unbearably complex, hazardous and obscure in outcome, the success of educational exchange is a beacon of hope." This book will, I believe, create a greater awareness of the existence of this beacon and, even more important, the tremendous potential to be achieved by increasing the candle power.

Mr. Coombs has done a real service to the nation by putting in perspective the almost unlimited possibilities of the human side of foreign affairs. This is a significant contribution to the effort to upgrade the educational and cultural aspects of foreign policy. I hope that his book will stimulate widespread discussion of this vital issue which has been neglected far too long. Many of my colleagues in the Congress will, I know, agree with his analysis and conclusions. Perhaps it may cause some of my colleagues, particularly those who have been in positions to affect the size of our programs through budgetary controls, to ponder the ultimate results of their frugality. It is a thorough, persuasive survey of the problems and the opportunities in this all-important field of international relationships.

Contents

THE FOURTH DIMENSION
OF FOREIGN POLICY:
EDUCATIONAL AND CULTURAL
AFFAIRS

Introduction—The Vantage Point

Any Washington newsman would gladly trade his gold fillings for license to rifle the Secretary of State's in-box. It overflows with "top secret" cables and other documents which could readily command tomorrow's headlines. But not all its contents are the stuff of which headlines are made. This applies, for example, to memoranda on educational and cultural affairs (unless, of course, a scandal is brewing or Mona Lisa is coming to town). Those in charge of cultural affairs in the State Department are never bothered with how to "manage the news." Their problem is how to manage to get some.

I have seen major international educational and cultural conferences get front-page attention for a whole week running in Tokyo, Addis Ababa and Santiago, yet little or no notice whatever in the American press. The reason, I suppose, is obvious. Almost everyone agrees that these activities are "good things to do," and in the long run perhaps even essential. But on a day-to-day basis they get brushed aside—not only in the press but in the high councils of government—by the pressure of current crises. They occupy, as it were, the quiet, calm and sunny side of foreign relations, not the dramatic, stormy side.

What really matters, however, is not the scarcity of headlines but that these educational and cultural activities, which have proliferated markedly since World War II and have become a potent new dimension of American foreign policy, still lack a clear rationale, coherence and adequate recognition. To the casual observer they seem a bewildering profusion of unrelated activities. Some important policy makers and legislators regard them as vitally important, while others view them with skepticism. The time has come to take stock of this new dimension of foreign policy and to put it in perspective. This book attempts to do just that.

A bit of recent history will explain the angle from which I shall view the subject. Soon after taking office President Kennedy made it clear that his administration intended to give greater emphasis to the human side of foreign policy. Our own history demonstrated, he said, that there was no better way for the United States to help today's new nations become free and viable societies "than by assisting them to develop their human resources through education." Similarly, he observed, "there is no better way to strengthen our bonds of understanding and friendship with older nations than through educational and cultural interchange."[1]

A larger private effort by universities, foundations and others was needed, the President observed, along with a stronger and more unified official effort. "This whole field," he said, "is urgently in need of imaginative policy development, unification and vigorous direction." He would look to the Secretary of State to provide government-wide leadership, and to aid him there would be for the first time an Assistant Secretary of State for Educational and Cultural Affairs.

The new Assistant Secretary soon undertook four main responsibilities: (1) to direct the State Department's own exchange programs; (2) to give policy guidance in this field to all federal agencies and help harmonize their efforts; (3) to exercise U.S. leadership on policies and programs of international organizations concerned with educational and cultural affairs; and (4) to foster increased cooperation between the government and the private sector.

From this particular observation post within the government—the desk of the Assistant Secretary—one sees in panorama the

[1] White House Press Release, February 27, 1961.

great variety of educational and cultural activities now going on under public and private auspices. It is from here, too, that one can best discern their contribution to the goals of American foreign policy. In any event, since it was my privilege to be the first incumbent, it is from this vantage point that I feel best qualified to describe the scene.

Always an exciting and satisfying assignment, it was also a complex and frequently baffling one. More than once I wished, unreasonably, that someone had supplied me at the outset with a comprehensive guidebook to the new job, complete with road maps. But it could not be written, of course, until the new office had gained experience. Having acquired perhaps a modicum of such experience and prepared the way for an able successor, I left the post anxious to try my hand at the draft of such a guidebook, which others could later improve.

With the generous encouragement of the Council on Foreign Relations and the Carnegie Corporation, and with the scholarly hospitality of The Brookings Institution—for all of which I am very grateful—what started as a memorandum has reached the proportions of a short book. But in spirit it is still a memorandum, addressed to the Secretary of State in the hope that he and his Assistant Secretary for Educational and Cultural Affairs might find it of some small help in carrying out their heavy responsibilities. I feel confident, however, that the Secretary would have no objection to others reading it over his shoulder. It is, after all, just as much their business as his. Indeed, the private sector is still very much the senior partner in this aspect of U.S. foreign relations, and unless the general public takes a large and direct hand in international cultural activities the government can accomplish little. In this aspect of foreign policy, more than in any other, the individual citizen or private organization can have a decided influence on the course of events.

Despite the major importance of private efforts in this field, however, I shall concentrate mainly on government's role, believing that if the government's own policies are clear and its efforts well coordinated, the private sector can be counted on to do a better and more comprehensive job. On the other hand, if the government is not clear where it is heading or fails to take these matters seriously enough, it can hardly expect private parties to do better. The two efforts are inextricably linked. For this reason government-private relations and the issue of what is government's proper role—always a complex question in a free and pluralistic society—are of particularly great concern in this area of foreign policy.

Six basic questions have suggested the outline for this book— questions to which the Secretary of State and all others must find the best answers they can to carry out their responsibilities well:

First, what is meant by "educational and cultural affairs," and why are they so important to the aims of American foreign policy today?

Second, how did today's policies, programs, and issues come about? What were their origins and their history?

Third, what is going on today in this field—who is doing what, how much, and where?

Fourth, what are other major nations doing in this field, and what can we learn from their experience?

Fifth, what does it all add up to? What have been the achievements and the shortcomings to be taken into account in the shaping of our future course?

Finally, and most important, where should we go from here? How can the quality, quantity and effectiveness of our national effort be strengthened? What role should government play, and how can this role be played well?

My answers to these questions, obviously, can be only tentative and incomplete, a point of departure for further exploration. They are, it should be emphasized, only one man's opinion.

I am anxious to acknowledge a deep debt of gratitude to the many individuals and organizations, too numerous to mention by name, who generously supplied me with facts and suggestions. I am especially indebted to my former colleagues in government, who served as my teachers, and to the wise and experienced men who gave generously of their thoughts and time as my advisory panel at the Council on Foreign Relations.

Needless to say, I accept full responsibility for all the views expressed. And lest there be any doubt, it should be emphasized that this book—written after I left the federal service and before I became an international civil servant—represents the private expression of an individual American to his own countrymen. To read more than that into it would be false. Despite these qualifications, however, I believe it can be fairly and fortunately said that in large measure these views do reflect an emerging consensus among people who have thought extensively about this important aspect of our foreign policy. If this book, by provoking open discussion and debate, helps to clarify the issues and to spur useful national action, it will have served its purpose well and proved a profitable exercise in the true spirit of educational and cultural endeavor.

Chapter I

The Underdeveloped Area of U.S. Foreign Policy

International educational, scientific and cultural relations are today a bewildering kaleidoscope—a colorful swirl of activities conducted by innumerable public and private agencies, all seemingly going it alone in different directions. Activities in this field make up a most motley assortment, including, for example, all kinds of exchanges of people—students, professors, technical experts and scientists, businessmen, athletes, government and civic leaders, ballet and theater companies, individual artists, performers and writers, and trainees in agriculture, industry and the military arts. They also include exchanges of "things," such as books and journals, films and TV programs, art and trade exhibits. The United States is engaged, moreover, in extensive programs of financial aid and technical assistance to help other nations develop their educational systems, their scientific research capabilities, and the knowledge and capacities of their people. Here at home there are new efforts to raise American competence in world affairs—for example, by improving the teaching of foreign languages and research on foreign areas.

What do all these activities have in common? Above all, what do they have to do with American foreign policy? It is the thesis of this book that they not only have a great deal to do with it but should take their place as a significant new dimension of foreign policy, on a parity with the more traditional political, economic and military dimensions. But this new dimension is still not fully recognized. Education and cultural relations remain an underdeveloped area of foreign policy.

I am aware that this thesis, although it already has many supporters as ardent as myself, will be doubted by two main groups of skeptics. One group believes foreign policy should confine itself to such "hard" and "realistic" matters as diplomacy, military strategy, and economic interests. Its adherents are unconvinced that better understanding between nations gives any assurance of better relations or that educational and cultural activities can make the slightest dent on the tough cold-war problems challenging the United States today. The other group comprises those engaged in educational and cultural pursuits who fear that any association of their works with foreign policy and government will sully their integrity and jeopardize freedom of inquiry and expression. This group, far from doubting that these activities can lend strong support to foreign policy, seems almost afraid that they will.

Both groups raise legitimate questions which deserve thoughtful answers. I believe the answers sketched in this book will show that to employ on behalf of America's essential long-term international objectives its great cultural and educational strengths, and to do so precisely by preserving their unique integrity and freedom, could constitute one of the major advances in American foreign policy in our era.

I am aware also that in government and elsewhere there is a certain ambivalence toward educational, scientific and cultural affairs. There is a widespread feeling, on the one hand, that here is something very basic and important; on the other, there is a too frequent failure to match good words with deeds. If my thesis is valid, it might reasonably be asked, how do I account for this skepticism and ambivalence? Why have we not before now developed this new dimension and given it a more prominent place in foreign policy?

The answer lies partly in its very complexity, diversity, and impreciseness, and in the sheer intellectual and administrative difficulty of bringing its scattered parts into orderly focus. But the answer lies also in the fact that our image of the world and our assumptions about it which shape our foreign policies have not yet fully caught up with the revolutionary changes that have swept the world in the past two decades. This is not to say that the response of American foreign policy to these changes has not been broad and deep and in itself revolutionary, for indeed it has been all of that. But much more remains to be done.

Foreign Policy in a World of Change

Since this book views its subject in the broad context of foreign policy and foreign relations, I should state at the outset what these terms mean to me and how I view the process by which they function. The foreign relations of the United States, the broader of the two terms, encompass all aspects of this nation's relationships with other nations and peoples: how they view us and behave toward us, how we view and act toward them, and what sorts of interactions occur. This complex of relationships is influenced by a host of factors, both governmental and private. It lies within the power of virtually any individual American or private organization to take part in and influence our foreign relations, sometimes quite seriously. A business firm or philanthropy, a missionary or movie producer, a novelist or artist, newsman or broadcaster, the family that provides hospitality to a foreign visitor are all examples of Americans who daily have an impact on foreign relations, for better or for worse.

Foreign policy, on the other hand, as I shall use the term, is what government does about our foreign relations in conscious pursuit of our national security, welfare, and specific goals with respect to individual countries (e.g., Cuba), or to groups of countries (e.g., the NATO members or the Communist bloc), or to the whole world. To be sure, there are the private policies of business corporations, foundations, and churches, for example, which affect American foreign relations. Sometimes these private policies are consistent with and helpful to the government's foreign policies, and at other times they are quite the reverse. At all times they must be taken into account. But I shall reserve the term foreign policy for the federal government, as does the Constitution—all else being designated "the private sector," even including for these purposes state and local governmental institutions.

This distinction between foreign policy and foreign relations has an important bearing upon the educational and cultural aspects of foreign policy. For, although government can make the official policies, it must in this field rely heavily upon the private sector to carry them out through voluntary action. As public and private policies will not necessarily coincide, the federal government and the private sector must somehow manage to be partners in this enterprise, even if at times uneasy ones.

The process by which our government makes foreign policy is neither a science nor an art; it is a highly pragmatic, intuitive process, usually conducted under great pressure of time and seldom with sufficient facts. The decisions and actions that emerge from this seemingly untidy process, however, are not random accidents. They have in fact a high degree of consistency and continuity, because they are shaped by a complex, durable and invisible structure of ideas, much as a new-born child is shaped by a hidden structure of genes and chromosomes.

This structure of ideas, premises and perceptions—through which our view of the world is filtered and from which our foreign policies are evolved—is fashioned from an accumulation of experience, knowledge, theories, prejudices and values which mirror the nation's background and aspirations. There is, in other words, an American "view" of the world and of our role in it, just as there is a French or Indian or Soviet "view" which shapes their foreign policies. This view is not static; it is strikingly different today from what it was in the 1930s. Yet it tends to change slowly, more slowly in times like these than the world itself, thus creating a gap between our perceptions of the world and its actual realities.

One aspect of this time-lag is the lingering influence of attitudes and theories which colored our national thinking of an earlier day, emphasizing moral principles, international law, or power relationships, as the case might be. Some reflected our own domestic experience; others, a concept based more on the nineteenth century system of nation-states than on the world of today. No theory of power, for example, explains how in the last fifteen years dozens of Asian and African colonies gained their independence from imperial nations despite conspicuous inferiority to them in all attributes of military and economic strength.

Obviously, U.S. foreign policy has not been imprisoned by any obsolete or doctrinaire theory. We have responded to new conditions in new ways that could not have been foreseen by an earlier generation. We adjust very rapidly when it suddenly develops, for example, that the Japanese have attacked Pearl Harbor or that the Soviets have placed missiles in Cuba. But there are many other important changes in the international environment—less dramatic and less immediately ominous ones—to which our thinking adjusts far less quickly, and sometimes too late. If the world has changed more than we realize, then our diagnoses and our prescriptions are likely to be deficient. A case in point is the greatly increased influence which people, ideas, and knowledge are exerting upon the course of world events today, compared to earlier generations, but which our foreign policy has not yet taken sufficiently into account.

Quite naturally we have given major attention since World War II to situations that most conspicuously called for action, above all the threat of Communist aggression. We have given priority to building military strength and placed heavy emphasis on economic reconstruction and development of other nations. We have seen, quite rightly, that our own security and the preservation of democratic freedom in the world depends heavily upon our own good economic health, on the strength of the whole Western world, and on substantial economic growth in the developing nations. But it is becoming increasingly clear that these military and economic measures, though unquestionably essential, are not adequate in themselves to cope with the real complexities of the world.

We have lately begun to speak, therefore, not only of economic development but also of social development. Though the latter term remains ill defined, its very use concedes that there is much more to fostering a free society than raising its gross national product. We are also aware, thanks partly to General de Gaulle's jolting reminders, that ties of political and economic interest or of mutual security among the advanced democratic nations can only be strong if they are built on something even stronger, namely, cultural and intellectual values and deep mutual understanding that can endure heavy weather. This is not to say that close ties and understanding will overcome all differences, particularly as nations such as France strive to regenerate their prestige and influence. But without them such nationalistic strivings can disastrously tear the fabric which holds the democratic world together.

The time has evidently come, then, not to reduce our efforts on the economic or the military side of foreign policy so long as danger persists, but to increase our effort on the human side, which, though not ignored, has received too little attention. A common fund of ideas and cultural understanding among the Western nations must undergird any common market for economic goods or any common effort toward security. In the developing countries the building of roads and dams and factories must be matched by the building of people and human relationships. The reason all this is so becomes evident as we scan the revolutionary changes that have swept the world in recent decades.

The affairs of mankind have been altered more in the lifetime of today's college freshman than in any previous hundred years of human history. This momentous change is the result of the confluence of several revolutions in our time, with their profound effect upon nearly every human endeavor and relationship.

One is the revolution of nationalism which, spreading from Europe to the far corners of the earth, has now more than doubled the number of independent nations (from 50 in 1945 to more than 120 in 1964) by dismantling, in less than two decades, great empires which took a century or more to build. Another is the demographic revolution which has enlarged the family of man with explosive speed so that if the present rate continues unabated, the world's population will double in only thirty-five years. A third is the revolution in science and technology with its promise of eradicating the ancient plagues of poverty, pestilence, and ignorance that have dogged man's trail through history and with its threat, too, of turning civilization to ashes in less than an hour. As H. G. Wells observed, civilization has become a race between education and disaster. Especially pertinent here are the new techniques of transportation and communication which have shrunk the globe, making close neighbors of formerly dark and distant continents and quickening the circulation of provocative ideas and knowledge throughout the world. It is said that Thoreau, when told that the first telegraph link had been completed between Maine and Texas, asked whether Maine had anything to say to Texas. With Telstar now in orbit, Thoreau's question must be seriously asked on a global scale.

A revolution of ideas, less tangible but no less potent, has rudely shaken traditional patterns of thought. Not all of them are new. Perhaps Americans today have forgotten the power of the ideas of their own revolution—liberty, equality, human rights, democracy, progress, the dignity of the individual, due process of law, the responsibility of government to promote the general welfare. But these ideas, carried now to the remotest nations and oppressed peoples, are shots still heard round the world. Answering shots from the Communist camp run the gamut from peaceful coexistence to violent revolution—depending on which capital is talking and what are the tactics of the moment. These ideas, often with the same labels as those of the West but with different meaning and intent, have an appeal to intellectuals and masses alike—especially among the economically less advanced peoples of the world—that should not be underrated. Those who have little reason to be happy with the old order in their own societies will listen to those who condemn it, who talk of liberating the downtrodden from further exploitation by landlords and capitalists and foreign imperialists, and eventually creating a new and peaceful order in which all men and all nations will be equal.

The most fertile and sometimes the most disruptive of these ideas on the loose is "progress." Common to all the "isms," it has for generations challenged the *status quo* in the Western world and now, like a genie from a bottle, it is roving the planet. Long-suffering masses in ancient static societies have suddenly been gripped by the once incredible notion that tomorrow can be better than today. Their insistence that this should really happen is giving restless nights to all in authority—governments, tribal chieftains, and landlords alike.

The revolution of ideas and the ideological contest between two very different approaches to the "good life" have sown danger and tensions in the developed world, and confusion and turmoil in the developing nations. Most of the latter are neither open nor closed societies. They are groping their way toward something as yet undefined, though certainly quite different from the traditional society of their past. Much as they want help and need it badly they want no part of the cold war. However myopic their view may seem to others, from their sidelines they see it as a struggle between two equally dangerous giants, which is none of their affair (a stance reminiscent of George Washington's advice to young America to give the ancient quarrels of Europe a wide berth). In the meantime the giants and their neighbors north of the equator have been preoccupied with the cold war to the point where perspectives become blurred and distorted.

Meanwhile, too, the old order has indeed changed and will continue to change with the widespread consequences of the several revolutions for almost every aspect of human life and society. The result of crucial significance to us here is the vastly increased role of people, ideas, and knowledge in world affairs and the effect it has had and must continue to have upon American foreign policy.

The highly charged compound of people, ideas, and knowledge, stirred by the new technologies and the ideological contest, has unleashed human drives far more powerful in their impact on societies and governments than the force of nuclear energy. In one country after another this compound has lately demonstrated its power to topple governments and defeat armies, to tear old cultures asunder and to start building new ones. Underestimated, if not ignored, for too long, it is writing the future history of Latin America, a part of our Western world, as it is writing that of Asia and Africa.

Millions of ordinary people who once accepted government as a superior authority to be paid and obeyed have now caught the radical notion that governments are meant not merely to rule but to serve. And to serve not just the privileged elites but the common people. Among these common people everywhere a consensus is crystallizing around a few simple but basic aspirations—peace, better living conditions, equality of opportunity, and human dignity—all brightly inscribed in the U.N. Charter. Superimposed is the ubiquitous drive for national self-assertion, not inscribed in the Charter.

Governments can ignore these aspirations only at their peril. Rulers, even in authoritarian societies, are becoming more sensitive and responsive to the opinions and needs of the ruled. They are also finding them harder to control. Governments honestly committed to serving the people's welfare are finding that their strongest tools for building viable independent societies are people and knowledge, and therefore that the precondition for over-all development is to develop the people themselves.

In short, it can be said that ideas and the knowledge of great numbers of people are shaping the behavior and fate of governments and the course of societies more than ever before. Equally important, they are also shaping the relationships among nations. The resulting transformation of diplomacy has become one of the facts of our times. Diplomacy can no longer be simply a dialogue between governments. For one thing, recognition of the growing leverage that the people now have upon their governments has prompted every major nation in the postwar period to use as an instrument of its diplomacy an elaborate overseas information service. One intent of these information services, to put it bluntly, is to talk right past foreign governments to their people in the hope of influencing the policies of those governments. What is said—truth or lies—varies with the motive.

The people, too, are increasingly taking diplomacy into their own hands. Their dialogue across national borders covers an ever-widening spectrum of subjects through business and labor, scientific cooperation, teaching and learning, books and the arts, film and radio and television. Even when such interchange is arranged by governments and narrowly confined, as for instance in the U.S.–U.S.S.R. exchange, it escapes the formal channels of diplomacy and provides new and more flexible approaches to broader understanding. Nowhere is the popular conviction that this is a sound and hopeful trend more evident than in the

United States. It provides the best explanation of why most of the major initiatives in the past eighteen years to inaugurate or strengthen cultural and educational exchange programs have had broad support in Congress. It explains also why those programs have had an impact all out of proportion to their size.

The strong inclination among peoples of the world to intercultural conversation—to be friendly and informal, to gain new insights and knowledge, to get along better than their governments often do—is making it increasingly difficult to keep closed societies closed and to keep mischievous misconceptions from dissolving in the solvent of truth. In this dialogue among peoples the free and open societies are at their greatest advantage. The advantage derives not only from the tradition of free speech and inquiry, but also from the evident benefits which the democratic and continuing revolution in such fields as industry, agriculture, and education have to offer the newly developing countries.

Some Americans, suffering from daily exposure to crisis headlines, are inclined to forget these great strengths that reside in our own long and honorable revolutionary tradition. They are impatient and fearful of the untidy, often noisy and disturbing turmoil arising from the revolutionary changes taking place elsewhere. In such an attitude they tend unwittingly to reinforce the propaganda line of others that the cold war is a contest between the defenders of the *status quo* (the United States and the West) and the promoters of change and progress (the Communist countries). The cold war, of course, is nothing of the sort; for as a practical choice the *status quo* does not stand a chance, nor would we want it to. The real choice lies between two kinds of revolution—one which brings about human progress and justice by means which respect law and order and human life, and the other which does not.

The Fourth Component of U.S. Foreign Policy

The response of American foreign policy to these world-wide revolutionary developments has itself been revolutionary. During and following World War II the people of the United States decided to turn away from their former isolationist course and to accept, even if reluctantly, the role of leadership thrust upon them—if for no other reason (though there were others) than to make the world safe for the United States. Inevitably this decision, reinforced by the unanticipated cold war, led to a vast expansion of international activities. To exercise leadership and secure its own interests the United States was obliged to broaden, deepen, and enormously strengthen the traditional economic, political, and military components of foreign policy and to add new dimensions.

Politically, reversing long tradition, we have gone internationalist, interventionist, and multilateral. Where earlier we clung to a policy of "noninvolvement," now we are the busy architects of "entangling alliances." We have discovered that even by *not* acting—by not financing a dam, for example, or recognizing a military junta, or supporting a commodity price, or mediating a distant dispute—we can profoundly influence the affairs of others. And learning from the unhappy lessons of turning our back on the League of Nations, we are now the host and largest supporter of the United Nations.

The economic component of our foreign policy, narrowly conceived in prewar days, has also grown beyond recognition through policies and programs of promoting trade, rendering aid, and supporting international economic stability. Today these policies and programs are a major factor in the world economy and in the economic life of many nations.

The enormously expanded military side of our foreign policy has been perhaps most dramatic of all. When we discovered, none too soon, that in 1945 the world had moved not from war to peace but from a hot war to a cold war, we reversed the hasty dismantling of our military establishment and ever since have given it top priority.

Whatever criticism one may make of this or that specific in the conduct of American foreign policy, its postwar record has certainly been a remarkably bold and creative one. The observable results are by now sufficiently encouraging to warrant a calmer confidence in the general correctness of its basic direction than we have at times shown. Yet clearly the time is far off when the scope and conduct of our international programs and policies will be so perfected, and the results so assured, that we can relax either our efforts or our fears. We must keep asking ourselves whether what we are doing is enough, whether our priorities are right and our total effort properly allocated between short- and long-run needs, between geographic areas, and between the different components of foreign policy; above all, whether we are drawing sufficiently upon *all* our relevant strengths. Literally everything we cherish is at stake, and since America's ability to influence world events is limited, as our resources inevitably are, we can ill afford to waste either strength or opportunity.

Such an assessment, I believe, will reveal an important "underdeveloped area" of foreign policy, an area where, though a strong beginning has been made, the United States is still falling substantially short of properly utilizing its ready capabilities. It is what I would characterize as the human side of foreign policy, and its proper development entails the necessary additional response that must be made by U.S. foreign policy if it is fully to adapt itself to, and capitalize on, the revolutions which have brought people, ideas, and knowledge to the forefront of international affairs. Its content, encompassing the wide range of educational, scientific and cultural activities already under way, is interwoven with the political, economic, and military aspects of foreign policy. Yet these activities have in themselves sufficient family resemblance and unity to warrant their own separate identity. Their common denominator is perhaps best, though imperfectly, expressed by the term "educational," for they embrace all those things having to do with the process and the stuff of learning, broadly conceived.

The human side of foreign policy is concerned, in short, with the development of people, both within and beyond our borders—their skills and knowledge, insights and understanding, attitudes and values, and all their creative potentialities. It is concerned also with the development of knowledge and creative works—with scholarly research and scientific discovery, with the cultivation of the arts and humanities. And it is concerned with the transmission and application of ideas and knowledge in myriad forms and ways.

Accordingly, I suggest that this whole family of international activities be called our foreign policy's "educational component," using the term broadly to include the wide assortment of programs listed in the first paragraph of this chapter. I have chosen this label with one misgiving, namely, that to many it may conjure up an image of classrooms, teachers and textbooks, whereas what I mean by it is obviously far more extensive than formal education. I hope this larger conception of education will be borne in mind throughout the discussion.

The tempting alternative is to call it the "cultural component," which some no doubt would prefer. I rejected this term reluctantly on three counts. It is, for one, even more ambiguous in English than the word "educational," meaning for some the fine and performing arts alone; and meaning for others, among them the sociologists, all the folkways, techniques, and values of a given society. Secondly, the term "cultural relations" has long been used to connote an aspect of diplomacy practiced by European nations which is considerably narrower in outlook than the educational component as defined here, and I should like to differentiate the two. Finally, there is the unhappy fact that in our society this excellent word "culture" is in some quarters its own worst enemy, as anyone will agree who has ever sought funds for "cultural affairs" from a congressional appropriations committee. There are still those who find it a less than manly word and deride the notion that anything wearing the label could possibly have important bearing on the serious business of foreign policy. (Even the British have their troubles with it. The London *Times* in 1934 congratulated the founders of the British Council for avoiding "culture" in its title. It was a word, the *Times* observed, which "comes clumsily and shyly off the Englishman's tongue.")

The resources which the educational component brings to the service of American foreign policy are those of great national vitality. They include our educational establishment, learned societies, and research institutes; the various academic disciplines and professions; our rich stockpile of technical and other knowledge; our creative artists, writers and performers, their past and present works and the institutions through which they function; our scientists, discoverers and inventors of every sort; in short, all our most creative brainpower, institutions, and achievements. Undergirding the structure are the talents and the generous and patriotic energies of ordinary citizens, frequently channeled through civic organizations toward public ends. The educational component more than any other affords abundant opportunity for private individuals and groups to participate directly in the nation's foreign relations. Much of importance that they can do, government by itself cannot do. These various resources, as much as our great industrial plant or our military power, are the well-springs of America's strength, the hallmark of its uniqueness, and much of what commands the respect and confidence of others.

Many people in the academic and artistic world may at first be put off by this blunt association of their work with foreign policy, fearful of being used as "political tools." If this were the issue—if it were a question of government, in order to attain narrow political purposes, attempting to "use" scholars and artists in ways that cast them out of character and compromised their integrity—I would share their fear. Anyone who believes in the basic values of our society is bound to oppose such tactics by government, for they would be not only wrong in principle but self-defeating in practice.

But this is not the case, and it is not the issue. It is important to avoid confusing the different meanings of "political," and to distinguish between long-range basic objectives and more narrow objectives which relate to a specific time and place. For many, politics is an invidious term, implying manipulation, double-talk, and sometimes downright deception. What the scholar fears is being made a manipulator of the truth, being trapped into reading the lines of some government propagandist—perhaps to convince some Asian intellectuals that how the United States voted in the United Nations last week was absolutely right (when he has his own doubts), or to assure an African leader that the racial situation at home is rosier than it really is, or to defend before some Latin American students the U.S. recognition of a military junta. He fears, in short, being put in the position of advocate for each and every U.S. policy and action and surrendering his right to speak the truth as he sees it.

Admittedly there are potential dangers here to be guarded

against, but I have yet to hear of any American scholar abroad who was urged by a U.S. government official to keep his criticisms to himself or to defend to foreigners any condition or policy of which he disapproved. Possibly there have been such incidents, but they are few and far between. Quite the opposite does happen occasionally, when seasoned foreign service officers have felt called upon to reassure an over-enthusiastic scholar on his first trip overseas that he really was not expected to defend the United States against every criticism or to win the cold war singlehanded.

But the real issue is not one of "using" private individuals to defend all U.S. policies, good or bad. It is rather a question of how best to reinforce the basic long-range objectives of U.S. foreign policy, which virtually all American scholars and artists would find no difficulty embracing with enthusiasm. To say that educational and cultural strengths should not be brought to the support of those objectives would be to argue that a free society should cope with the world with its strong right arm tied behind it.

Transcendent among these long-range goals, in the late President Kennedy's words, is to achieve "a peaceful world community of free and independent nations, free to choose their own future and their own system, so long as it does not threaten the freedom of others." This goal, however, must be approached through a combination of more specific objectives. Paramount and most urgent of these is to prevent aggressive forces anywhere from upsetting the peace and destroying freedom. It is to this end that our enormous military investment and many daily diplomatic negotiations are directed; and without success here, nothing else will matter.

But such efforts are essentially negative in purpose, in the sense that they are meant to buy time and opportunity for more positive approaches. It is to these positive approaches that educational and cultural endeavors can make their greatest contribution. Specifically, they can help accomplish, in combination with other measures, the major aims that are bound to preoccupy American foreign policy for a long time to come: to forge greater strength and unity within the community of the developed democratic nations; to assist the developing nations in their efforts toward modernization and toward becoming viable, independent societies; to expand the area of mutual interest, understanding, and cooperation and to reduce the explosive tensions between the Western and the Communist worlds in the search for an acceptable basis for making coexistence not merely a slogan but a reality; to strengthen the international machinery for keeping the peace and advancing human welfare; and to knit together the world community and enrich the lives of human beings.

How educational and cultural relations can best be utilized to support these large objectives—country by country, activity by activity, and agency by agency—is a matter for later consideration. Here, two general ways may be indicated. One is by fostering a broader and deeper understanding of America on the part of other nations and peoples, so that this nation's policies and behavior will be understood more accurately and sympathetically, and its leadership thereby applied more effectively. The other way is by enlarging American understanding of other nations and our general competence in world affairs, so that our policies and leadership will be better informed, widely supported at home, and more effective abroad.

It is important to understand that the educational side of foreign policy is not a panacea or a substitute for other activities now going on. But the political, economic and military approaches have each their limitations. The educational component can in many ways reinforce them and, imaginatively employed, can accomplish things beyond their reach, adding fresh vitality, depth, and flexibility to American foreign policy.

Much is already going on in this "underdeveloped" area, as the next two chapters demonstrate. The United States has by no means been blind to the human side of foreign policy. Our deficiencies lie less in the *quantity* of the national effort—though there are important deficiencies here—than in its *quality*, in its disorder, and in its lack of clear purpose.

We have, in short, the building materials for a strong educational component, but we have not yet created the architectural design. Until the pieces are fitted together more rationally and related to clear-cut national objectives, they will continue to look like a colorful but patternless quilt. They will be regarded as a mixture of unrelated "good things to do" but hardly taken seriously, and they will contribute far less than they could to a stronger nation and a saner world.

Chapter II

How Did Today's Issues Develop?

The United States first added an educational-cultural dimension to its foreign policy on the eve of World War II, mainly to counter the Nazi cultural offensive in Latin America. In the ensuing twenty-five years this endeavor has greatly expanded in size, geographic scope, variety, and purpose. With this growth several crucial and often troublesome issues have persisted like hardy perennials. Occasionally they have been settled by some new law or policy declaration, but only to become unsettled again or resolved in the opposite direction by a shift in the tide of international events, national politics, or administrative leadership.

Since the issues are still much alive today and will recur throughout this account, it will be useful at the outset to list them and some further questions they raise:

1. Should educational and cultural activities—at least those sponsored or supported by the federal government—be consciously aimed at foreign policy objectives? Or should they be treated as ends in themselves, best divorced from foreign policy?

2. Should educational and cultural programs be intermingled with foreign information activities ("propaganda") or sharply divorced from them? Is there, in fact, a clear distinction?

3. How should government and private efforts be related?

4. What is government's proper role, given the fact that most of

our society's educational and cultural resources lie outside the federal government and beyond its direct control?

5. What is the relationship of educational and cultural exchange programs to technical assistance and aid for economic development? Do they have different missions, or are they part and parcel of the same thing?

6. What relative emphasis should the United States give to bilateral and multilateral efforts in this field, and how should the two be related? Is there presently a serious imbalance in the division of national effort through these two channels?

7. How much should the U.S. government spend on this component of foreign policy compared, say, to the economic and military components; and how should it be financed?

8. How should government activities in this whole field be organized and administered to insure unity of direction and maximum efficiency and effectiveness?

The Start in the War Years

Cultural relations with foreign countries, of course, did not begin in 1938 when the U.S. government, the last of the great powers to do so, took the decision to enter that field, which from the earliest colonial days had been left almost exclusively in private hands.[1]

These private interchanges, it should be emphasized, played a major role in developing a robust nation from a raw continent. From the very beginning, the United States was a net cultural importer from the "old world," receiving educated people, a vast inventory of knowledge and arts, and political, philosophical, religious and economic ideas. Only in recent decades has this "balance of trade" been reversed, with the United States becoming a net cultural exporter. But even now, as a so-called advanced nation, this country remains a large cultural importer, helping to sustain thereby its own dynamic. One of American history's most

[1] The reader interested in fuller details about the historical background of the U.S. government's educational and cultural effort will find, as I have, two books especially helpful: Ruth McMurry and Muna Lee, *The Cultural Approach—Another Way in International Relations* (Chapel Hill: University of North Carolina Press, 1947), which covers the period up to 1946; and Charles A. Thompson and Walter H. C. Laves, *Cultural Relations and U.S. Foreign Policy* (Bloomington: Indiana U. Press, 1963), covering the full period to 1961.

important lessons for the new nations of today—and for those trying to help them—is that without these cultural imports, and without a prodigious educational investment of its own, the United States would never have become a major world power.

The circumstances prevailing before 1938 changed abruptly when Hitler set his course on conquest and chose cultural weapons, among others, for the purpose. The U.S. government, forced to abandon its hands-off position, adopted a policy of supplementing and stimulating private cultural intercourse. The war years that followed planted the seeds of almost every present-day federal program of international education, science, culture, technical assistance, and information, and saw the rise of most of the critical and complex issues listed above.

Hitler's perversion of cultural relations to aggressive ends, his export of strident German nationalism and racism, gave early alarm to the British and French while the United States still slept. The creation of the British Council in 1934 was a direct result. A spokesman for the French Foreign Ministry in 1936 equated cultural relations with national defense. "At a time when it is necessary for us," M. Léon Archimbaud said, "to make the greatest sacrifices for the Army, the Navy, and military aviation, to prepare for a war which may be imposed upon us, there should be no penury in giving to the Ministry of Foreign Affairs, the outpost of National Defense, the necessary [cultural] means to safeguard peace."[2] When war finally came, the competition for world opinion grew sharper and official cultural activities expanded, along with propaganda. The British were strict in keeping the two sharply divorced, but both were intended to serve the ends of foreign policy and the war effort.

Across the ocean the American cabinet heard a stern warning in 1938 from President Franklin D. Roosevelt (a sailor who sensed the gathering storm sooner than most of his countrymen) that the time had come to batten the hatches in Latin America against the Nazi gale. Two actions followed which, as it turned out, made educational and cultural affairs irrevocably a component of American foreign policy. A Division of Cultural Rela-

2 McMurry and Lee, cited, p. 28.

tions was created in the State Department, which, with much private help, embarked on an effort to support Roosevelt's "good neighbor policy." The effort included exchanges of students, professors and specialists, support to American-sponsored schools in Latin America, book translations, libraries, cultural broadcasts, and educational films. An Interdepartmental Committee on Cooperation with the American Republics was also created to harness the resources of specialized federal agencies for improving the welfare of Latin Americans through technical assistance in agriculture, labor, communications, public health, education, and public administration.

Both actions implemented agreements reached in earlier inter-American conferences, and Congress sanctioned them in August 1939 with Public Law 355. This was to remain the government's chief mandate for educational, cultural and technical assistance activities until the Smith-Mundt Act provided a broader one, nine years later.

These early Latin American programs were financially modest by today's standard, but they did not want for talent and enthusiasm. President Roosevelt's personal interest insured government-wide cooperation at the highest levels, and Vice President Henry A. Wallace and various cabinet members participated in the venture personally. The new Cultural Relations Division, with its policy of using private channels wherever possible, enjoyed access to the nation's educational and cultural leaders and organizations. It turned, for example, to the Institute of International Education to handle student exchanges, the American Council on Education to assist American-sponsored schools in Latin America, and the American Library Association to create libraries and distribute books.

The outbreak of war in Europe in 1939 accelerated these efforts. The Office of the Coordinator for Inter-American Affairs was created in 1940, and President Roosevelt encouraged its energetic head, Nelson Rockefeller, to freewheel beyond the State Department's cautious constraints. The Rockefeller group paid chief attention to "information," through press, radio, and motion pictures, but gave a strong push as well to such cultural activities as art exchanges, book translations (in both directions), libraries, and exchanges of persons.

The Office of War Information (OWI), established in 1942 under the widely esteemed Elmer Davis, carried on a world-wide psychological warfare campaign outside Latin America. Its emphasis, too, was on "information"—news and "fast media"—but OWI likewise moved into books, libraries, and exchanges of journalists and other "opinion molders" to promote and supplement its propaganda wares.

In contrast to the British practice, this blending, by the Davis and Rockefeller offices, of education and culture with information and propaganda became a cause of controversy. Spokesmen for education and the arts, inside and outside government, insisted that they should be kept "pure" by being divorced from either propaganda or specific foreign policy objectives. The psychological warriors, however, had no qualms about using every weapon at hand, and in the circumstances theirs was the stronger voice.

Viewed in retrospect, this debate had an unreal and at times almost absurd quality. The same words meant different things to the adversaries. Yet it was a wholesome, necessary, and indeed inevitable debate for a democratic society which had long been shielded by happy circumstance from the hard and often ugly realities of world politics. The time had now arrived when the nation's educational and cultural strengths must come to the support of its international position. The debate was over how best to accomplish this without destroying the very values which national policy sought to preserve.

In any event the wartime educational and cultural effort was dwarfed by the information programs, which were more closely tied to the war itself. In the fast media against the slow and the short-run versus the long, it was a case of dollars against pennies. Despite all the talk, in the seven years from 1939 to 1946 only 800 Latin American students, fewer than 450 specialists, and 25 professors came north under government programs while only some 175 U.S. students and professors and about 50 technical experts visited Latin America. These small streams, nonetheless, set the course for larger future flows.

V-J Day in 1945 found the American people eager to remove all manifestations of war with almost thoughtless haste. Some were anxious to return to their old "normalcy," and others to get started building a brave new world. Virtually all assumed that the wartime allies, including the Soviet Union, would stick together to prevent the resurgence of aggression and to build the foundations of peace. In hope and idealism the United States led in creating the United Nations at San Francisco and soon afterward in establishing the United Nations Educational, Scientific and Cultural Organization (UNESCO), endorsing the latter's cardinal premise that prevention of war must begin "in the minds of men."

Responding to the popular mood, the new Truman administration lost no time dismantling the wartime emergency agencies, including OWI and the Office of the Coordinator. By late 1945 their remnants were consolidated with the Division of Cultural Affairs in the State Department. William Benton, dynamic former advertising executive, vice-president of the University of Chicago, and publisher of the *Encyclopaedia Britannica,* was named Assistant Secretary of State to preside over this household. His challenge was to organize the first U.S. peacetime information, educational and cultural programs—if indeed there were to be such, which was doubtful.

It is hard now to recall how utterly unenthusiastic, indeed downright hostile, the American people and Congress then were to the very idea of government being in the foreign information business in peacetime. Psychological warfare, like mass killing, had been accepted as a necessity of war; but "the dirty business of propaganda," as it was called, had no place in peacetime. There was no real need for it, the argument ran; information was the job of private newspapers and wire-services, not the business of government. There was fear, too, that propaganda machinery in government hands might be turned to manipulating public opinion in our own country.

Benton, supported by General George C. Marshall, then Secretary of State, fought a hard uphill battle from 1945 to 1947 to get new legislation and funds. Congress was in no hurry to grant fresh legislative authority. At one point the House chopped the

State Department's budget request for its information program from $31 million to zero, but a friendlier Senate saved the day. In the end, Benton and his colleagues won the battle, but only with the help of a new war, this one called "cold."

The Fulbright Amendment and the Smith-Mundt Act

Educational and cultural activities—to which no one was seriously opposed (as long as the costs were low)—suffered from guilt by association with the controversial information program, being in the same budget and organization. Yet, while the information battle raged, in 1946 Congress approved without serious controversy the so-called Fulbright Amendment and U.S. membership in UNESCO. More by accident than design, these two actions ushered the nation into a new era when educational and cultural activities would serve not merely as temporary expedients of war but as long-range elements in a strategy of peace.

One reason, no doubt, for favorable congressional action was that these measures had a peaceful ring which the American people were then most anxious to hear. But it is also a fact that most Congressmen were quite unaware of the full implications of the Fulbright Amendment. Its young sponsor, a Rhodes Scholar and former president of the University of Arkansas, astutely drew as little attention as possible to the measure as it ground through the legislative mill. Years later he told his Senate colleagues, "It was almost as if the words 'educational exchanges' were something that had to be sneaked into this historic building through the back door. . . ."[3]

Fulbright's innocuous-sounding amendment to the Surplus Property Act of 1944 authorized the Department of State to use government-owned foreign currencies from war surplus sales to finance the sending of American students abroad for "studies, research, instruction and other educational activities" and to defray transportation costs of foreign students coming to American colleges and universities. It was a financially painless measure; it asked no new tax dollars and simply proposed using in a good

[3] *Congressional Record,* June 27, 1961, p. 10580.

cause some of the foreign currencies piling up in war-torn countries.

The Fulbright program, as it soon came to be called, fitted perfectly the spirit of the times. International-minded academic and civic groups saw in it an appealing and practical means to promote world understanding. As hundreds of scholars began criss-crossing the ocean the very name Fulbright became a world-wide symbol of mutual understanding. At the program's fifteenth anniversary in 1961, President Kennedy called it "the classic modern example of beating swords into plowshares." By then there were exchange agreements with forty-four countries and over 45,000 American and foreign "Fulbright alumni." Few if any U.S. government efforts had ever gained such world-wide approval.

Its success was attributable partly to the administrative ground rules. The Fulbright program's policies and selections were governed by a distinguished "Board of Foreign Scholarships," and college faculties participated extensively in the selection process, which made it seem more the property of the academic community than of government. The fact that eminent foreigners sat on the binational selection commissions abroad was undeniable proof of the program's impartiality and nonpolitical character.

Yet for all its virtues the Fulbright program had limitations that became increasingly serious with time. It was restricted to academic exchanges, and it could operate only in countries where the U.S. government happened to own "excess" foreign currencies, which excluded a good many countries. It could cover only the transportation costs of foreign students, not their dollar costs in the United States, which had to be raised from private sources. And eventually its reserves of foreign currencies would be exhausted. In short, it was a good start but no more.

Early in 1948, with the Fulbright program well under way, Congress, under Benton's prodding, enacted the United States Information and Educational Exchange Act. Sponsored by Representative (now Senator) Karl Mundt and Senator H. Alexander Smith, this omnibus measure authorized both a world-wide information program and, to complement the Fulbright program, a broad educational exchange program funded by dollars. Its passage involved a longer and more acrimonious debate than the controversial Taft-Hartley Act of the same year.

Ironically, though the Smith-Mundt Act's language reflected earlier peaceful assumptions, it owed its passage to the new cold war. Many Congressmen had gone overseas in 1946 and 1947, and most came home shocked and angered by the calculated misrepresentations of the United States they had encountered and deeply concerned by the evident lack of understanding of American society and motives, even among good friends. Reluctantly they conceded the need for a continuing overseas information program.

In passing the Smith-Mundt Act, Congress gave much attention to most of the troublesome issues listed earlier. For one thing, it distinguished sharply between information and educational activities and insisted that the two be kept separate. In the congressional debate, the information program was variously described as "the psychological approach," "propaganda" and "public relations," designed to gain understanding and acceptance of U.S. policies abroad. Educational exchanges, on the other hand, were characterized by such terms as "cooperative," "mutual understanding" and "reciprocal" and were seen as having longer-range and more general objectives. "To be truly effective," Senator Smith insisted, the educational exchange program "must be objective, non-political, and above all, have no possible propaganda activities." It was a clear victory for those who had argued during the war for a clean separation.

On the issue of government-private relations, the Smith-Mundt Act expressly directed maximum use of private facilities and barred federal agencies from any activities that could be equally well performed by private groups. Although the Act did not deal directly with the issue of the bilateral versus the multilateral approach, it did, interestingly enough, specify that "information concerning the participation of the United States in the United Nations, its organizations and functions, shall be emphasized." This was a sign of the times that probably could not have been repeated in later years.

Reflecting these policies, the Smith-Mundt Act provided for an *information service* "to disseminate abroad information about the United States, its people, and policies" that would promote "a better understanding of the United States in other countries," and a separate *educational exchange service* "to cooperate with other nations in the interchange of persons, knowledge and skills; the rendering of technical and other services; and the interchange of developments in the field of education, the arts, and sciences." It is noteworthy that Congress regarded technical assistance as an integral part of the educational exchange program.

In carrying out the information program, the Secretary of State was authorized to use press, publications, radio, motion pictures, and other information media, as well as information centers. Under the educational exchange program he could "provide for interchanges on a reciprocal basis—of students, trainees, teachers, guest instructors, professors, and leaders in fields of specialized knowledge or skill," the interchange of books and periodicals, the translation of such writings, and the preparation, distribution and interchange of other educational materials. He was empowered to make grants of money, services and materials to schools, libraries and community centers abroad, founded or sponsored by American citizens, and to individuals and public or private nonprofit organizations in the United States or elsewhere. Most important of all, he could ask Congress to provide hard dollars for all these purposes.

The Cold War

These tools of peace were soon to become weapons in a cold war which, by the spring of 1950, had become brisk. President Truman, on the advice of Edward Barrett, an able newspaperman who succeeded Benton, called for a "Campaign of Truth" to combat Communist propaganda. He asked Congress to treble the information budget, and when the Communists invaded Korea that June Congress needed little prodding.

The earlier information policy advocated by Benton, of giving other peoples "a full and fair view" of the United States, now became an aggressive, hard-hitting, and at times a shrill anti-Communist campaign. The psychological warfare spirit and techniques of the old OWI days were revived in a new crusade against a new enemy. Priority was given to broadcasts behind the iron curtain; overseas libraries were renamed "information centers"; the translation of "politically effective" books was stepped up; "target groups" in countries of highest "strategic importance" were designated and given priority. The language of psychological warfare, mixed with the jargon of journalism, public relations and Madison Avenue pervaded the effort, the underlying premise of which was that words were weapons.

In this new cold war context the educational exchange program was soon outranked by the information program and increasingly became its handmaiden. Emphasis shifted to grants and exchanges which could have a "quick impact." A State Department reorganization—aimed at giving the information program greater freedom from the Department's hobbling bureaucratic constraints—classified exchange-of-persons programs and libraries as "media services," in the same category as radio, press, and motion pictures. Friends of the educational exchanges complained bitterly, but in vain.

These trends reached a climax early in the new Eisenhower administration when all overseas information activities were transferred from the State Department to a new semi-independent United States Information Agency. In the process the educational exchange programs were all but forgotten. Only by the intervention of an influential group, headed by Senator Fulbright and including Senators Mundt and Hickenlooper, were they kept from being placed under the new information agency. These objectors feared that there they would be dominated by the "psychological approach."

A compromise was reached which split the educational and cultural programs somewhere down the middle. Books, libraries, cultural centers, English-teaching, and exhibits went to USIA, while exchange-of-persons programs, support of American-sponsored schools, the UNESCO National Commission secretariat, and a few odds and ends were left behind in the State Department. The rationale for this strange division was that State would handle "cultural relations" while USIA handled "cultural information"—regarded by some at the time as a distinction without a difference which might have amused medieval metaphysicians.

It was in any event a Pyrrhic victory for the Fulbright group, or perhaps better a Potomac victory, since in the reshuffle the cultural affairs officers who handled State's exchange programs in the field, where it really counted, ended up under the USIA. There they would serve as part-time "field agents" for State, with two Washington bosses, but on the USIA payroll and promotion ladder and under the jurisdiction in each embassy of the Public Affairs Officer whose first loyalty was to USIA and whose first concern was its information program. Under this compromise solution, those pursuing the two approaches—the educational-cultural and the psychological—were to live apart in Washington but together in the field. It seemed a sure-fire formula for perennial discord, and so indeed it proved to be. But there was sufficient accommodation on either side to make the arrangement viable. It has survived to this date.

The Exchange Programs Struggle Along

The exchange programs that were left behind in the State Department were not unlike abandoned orphans. They had to make their way in a large bureaucratic maze whose procedures, attitudes, and prestige symbols were ill-designed to accommodate these operational programs. It was enough to frustrate even their hardiest supporters.

For administrative convenience the various units of the educational and cultural program were lumped in a loose federation called the International Educational Exchange Service (IES), under the Assistant Secretary for Public Affairs whose first concern, inevitably, was the Department's domestic press and public relations. To complicate matters further, IES was organized according to categories rather than on a geographic basis. Each of its relatively autonomous units was responsible on a world-wide scale for a particular exchange category (e.g., foreign students, American students, foreign leaders and specialists, U.S. specialists, American schools abroad, and the like). Each ran its own show more or less independently, worked out its own procedures, communicated separately with cultural officers in the field (which was rather confusing for them), and competed for shares of the budget.

There was no provision for strong central planning and policy direction which would insure the integration of these separate pieces, either in Washington or in the field. Nor were they closely related to other federal activities and to the evolving needs and objectives of U.S. foreign policy. It was virtually impossible for the personnel of each small unit to become really expert on every geographic area. Hence there was a natural tendency for each to develop its own standardized procedures and apply them in all areas of the world, rather than exploit the inherent flexibility of such programs to match the unique conditions and opportunities presented by each country. Under the circumstances the inevitable happened—means increasingly became ends in themselves, and a bad case of "hardening-of-the-categories" set in.

Throughout most of the Eisenhower era IES and the exchange programs suffered from these organizational ailments and from lack of high-level administrative, budgetary and political support. Promising young foreign service officers regarded IES as a career dead-end, to be avoided like the plague, and indeed the evidence justified their fears. The programs were kept alive and moving ahead mainly by a dedicated corps of civil servants, most without overseas experience, who were content to make what they considered an exciting and worthy career in this field. Much of the time they traveled a lonesome road.

Meanwhile, world-wide demands on the exchange program were expanding steadily throughout the 1950s, due especially to the proliferation of new nations in Africa and Asia. But financial resources did not proliferate, and a progressively wider "exchange gap" resulted. Top State Department officials, preoccupied with more immediately urgent budget needs, were not prone to fight for the exchange program—even though they had good words for it—when the Bureau of the Budget and the House Sub-Committee on Appropriations insisted, as they always did, on keeping a tight lid on the Department's over-all appropriation. The exchange budget, a sizable part of the Department's total budget because IES was the only grant-making operational unit, became the perennial area of compromise. Cuts that could not be made elsewhere could always be made there. The Senate Appropriations Committee, where there were some strong friends of the program, usually managed to restore a portion of the heavy losses suffered in the House. ("They call it the upper house," a member of the House Committee once complained to me, "because they always 'up' expenditures after we have tried to protect the taxpayer.")

The result was that dollar appropriations for the exchange program declined from $16 million in 1951 to less than $10 million by 1955 and did not recover until 1959. This shrinkage was only partially offset by a rise in foreign currency appropriations. The total of American and foreign grantees fell from more than 7,200 in 1951 to fewer than 4,900 in 1954 and rose only gradually from there on. While these cutbacks were being made, the number of countries participating in the programs rose from 62 in 1951 to 97 in 1959, forcing a progressively thinner spreading of the limited resources.

Despite these depressing fortunes, the exchange program managed to sustain considerable vigor and variety. For example, among the 4,600 foreign visitors in 1958 were: two delegations of Chilean legislators wishing to examine our political system; the Chief Justice of Ghana who came to study our judicial system (with the help of Chief Justice Earl Warren); a group of Tunisian educators studying American educational ideas at the University of Southern California; the editors of two large Indian newspapers, wanting to see what America was really like; a Korean university president who came to arrange for his faculty to be improved by study in the United States; five French legislators studying industrial productivity; the head of the Women's Division of the Icelandic Social Democratic Party, here to observe the role of American women in politics and public affairs. "Our Thai students doing graduate studies in the United States," the Prime Minister of Thailand wrote that year, "have not only bettered themselves, but have added to the human resources of our country."

During the 1950s, though the exchange program languished, further dimensions were added to U.S. foreign policy that were directly related to its educational side. One was "Point Four." The first three points in President Truman's inaugural address of January 1949 called for grim cold-war actions. But the fourth one set forth a proposition which promptly aroused humanitarian instincts and stimulated thought in many quarters. It involved essentially the same idea of technical assistance which had been applied during the war in Latin America and later authorized by the Smith-Mundt Act. But the "Point Four" proposal, approved by Congress in 1950, was more explicitly linked to the goal of over-all economic development in emerging nations and was far bolder in its global proportions.

Until then technical assistance had been viewed as an aspect of educational exchange. With a few amendments the Smith-Mundt Act could have provided adequate legal authority for the Truman proposal, and theoretically its administration could have been assigned to IES. But realistically, even beyond the annoying fact that the Smith-Mundt Act had been passed by that "do-nothing 80th Congress," the Point Four effort would clearly enjoy greater popular support and operational vigor if founded on new legislation and executed by a new agency with a fresh staff. Thus the Technical Cooperation Administration (TCA) was created as a semi-autonomous unit within the State Department independent of the existing exchange program.

Thereafter TCA and IES went their separate ways, in Washington and overseas. Semantical distinctions were created to justify the division. The foreign aid program claimed the mission of "helping other nations develop their indigenous strengths," while the exchange program fostered "mutual understanding." The personnel of both were quick to disavow, often vehemently and with deep conviction, any relationship between their programs and "political" objectives. The USIA, meantime, saw its mission as "improving America's image abroad" and made no bones about being a promoter of U.S. foreign policies and political objectives. Like three imperial powers these agencies kept the peace, despite occasional skirmishes, by respecting and avoiding each other's sphere of influence.

In reality, of course, these three missions were highly interdependent and needed careful blending. The aid program inevitably had a deep impact on "America's image abroad" and on "mutual understanding"; it was heavily involved with what were really educational exchanges and, despite wholehearted denials, with "political objectives." Conversely, the exchange program often contributed to "developing other nations' internal strengths" and certainly affected other people's conceptions of American society, sometimes more deeply than the USIA's mass media programs. But to insiders in each agency, anxious to avoid bureaucratic conflicts or invite outside intervention, there was a strong compulsion to keep these missions "exclusive" and to ignore their interdependence. From the Bureau of the Budget's point of view, these distinctions helped keep the bureaucratic organization chart tidy. The inevitable result, however, was the creation of a series of stubborn roadblocks to any effective integration of the federal government's entire effort in the educational and cultural field.

Financing remained a problem, despite unexpected new sources of foreign currency. Friends of the educational exchange program in Congress seized opportunities to expand its financial base by giving it access to various funds owed the United States by other nations—for example, by Finland for a post-World War I reconstruction loan and by India for the 1951 emergency wheat loan. The most important such measure by far was PL 480 (the Agricultural Trade Development and Assistance Act of 1954) which authorized foreign currencies, generated by overseas sales of U.S. surplus agricultural products, to be used for educational exchanges, American studies abroad, American-sponsored schools and colleges, libraries and community centers, and for the translation, publication and distribution of books and periodicals abroad.

Though a boon to the program, PL 480 was not an unmixed blessing. Congress developed the habit of relying on the generous supplies of these inconvertible foreign currencies which could be spent in only one country—"wooden nickels" some called them—without making enough dollar funds available to balance them in the many countries where local currency supplies were lacking. This produced geographic distortions and inflexibilities in the world-wide pattern of the exchange program and made for a feast-or-famine situation. Expenditures were heavy in certain countries (such as India and Egypt) where the U.S. government happened to own large supplies of unused local currencies, but very inadequate elsewhere, as in Africa and Latin America, where the program depended on dollars and where U.S. commitments were expanding rapidly. Moreover, when available local currency supplies ran out (as they did, for example, in Turkey), the exchange program had to be cut back abruptly, creating difficulties. To complicate matters, the Bureau of the Budget, partly fearing the inflationary impact in developing countries of an unbridled use of accumulated PL 480 funds, began to impose tight controls which further restricted the flexibility of the educational exchange program. The foreign currency situation eventually grew so complex that few people in government really understood it.

In Response to the Soviet Challenge

In the early 1950s the mounting "Soviet cultural offensive," as Professor Frederick Barghoorn has called it, brought concern to the Eisenhower administration. The Soviet government was making increasing use of touring ballets, orchestras, traveling circuses and the like to demonstrate its cultural accomplishments and peaceful intentions, and by indirection reinforcing the image of America as a materialistic, uncultivated society, interested only in gadgets, money, and exploitation.

To meet this competition President Eisenhower allocated emergency funds to supplement the normal commercial flow of American performing groups abroad and particularly to strengthen U.S. participation in international festivals. The need was greatest in Asia, Africa, and much of Latin America, where people were least informed about American artistic achievements and where U.S. musical, dance and theatre groups could not hope to make a commercial success. Congress in 1956 enacted the International Cultural Exchange and Trade Participation Act, which authorized the State Department to send "cultural presentations" abroad and the Department of Commerce to insure more adequate U.S. participation in international trade fairs.

The performing arts, however, constituted a singularly awkward subject for U.S. bureaucrats to cope with and soon became a political storm center. Skeptics and unfriendly critics of the exchange program as a whole—a handful of Congressmen and columnists—found easy sport in making the cultural presentations program their target.

Notwithstanding such criticism the administration took the decision to go ahead, and even to start exchanges with the Soviet Union itself where certain evidences of a thaw had appeared since Stalin's death. President Eisenhower had himself engaged in person-to-person diplomacy with Bulganin and Khrushchev at the summit conference in 1955. One of their main agreements was that the United States and the Soviet Union should strengthen their mutual educational and cultural relations. The follow-up was slow, but finally in January 1958 the first Soviet-American Exchange Agreement was signed.

The fact that an agreement could be reached at all meant that each party felt it had more to gain than to lose by exchanges, though each obviously had quite different motives. Soviet leaders wanted to convince the American public that the Soviet Union deserved better than the distrust and antagonism shown it by the American government and its Western allies. In line with their proclaimed policy of "peaceful coexistence," they hoped to soften U.S. opposition to Soviet policies generally. They also wanted fuller access to the useful technical knowledge and experience of the United States which could be applied profitably to their own growing society. And it was only prudent, many felt, to assume that the Soviets also hoped to use the exchange program for espionage and subversion if they got a chance, but the subsequent record on this score did not prove alarming.

The United States, for its part, hoped for beneficial effects on Soviet attitudes and policies, and in the long run on Soviet society itself, by lifting the iron curtain and exposing the Soviet people to external influences. This might be accomplished, it was felt, by communicating directly with the Soviet people through various forms of exchange not especially concerned with politics but with matters of common and genuine interest. In the process Soviet citizens might discover that American society was not as black as it had been painted by their government and indeed had appealing virtues—not least of them freedom of individual inquiry and expression. There was a strong desire, too, especially among American scholars, to learn more about the Soviet Union —its history, institutions, progress and problems, and what really made it tick.

Agreement provided for a variety of exchanges on a modest scale: students, professors, and research scholars; technical teams from industry, agriculture, education, health, and the like; athletes and artistic performances; books and magazines; films and television broadcasts. The exchanges were thereafter carried out with strict reciprocity—a team for a team, a Benny Goodman for a Leningrad Orchestra, and a travel restriction for a travel restriction.

Though basic negotiations have been handled on the American side by the State Department, the actual exchanges have been largely financed and carried out by private organizations— university committees, foundations, industrial associations, and commercial impresarios. These private U.S. groups, of course, have no real counterparts in the Soviet Union. Their initiatives and their independence of the U.S. government, which many Soviet visitors first found hard to believe, may well be one of the most beneficial features of the program.

The original agreement has since been renewed, at two-year intervals, with moderate expansion and liberalization. On each occasion both parties, though presenting long lists of complaints, agreed that on the whole the exchange was proving useful and should be continued.

The Soviet challenge has also made itself felt in other ways. The national shock and mortification produced by the first Soviet Sputnik brought an outcry against the deficiencies of American education. However dubious the logic of attributing the Soviet space success to the shortcomings of American public schools, it did produce some long overdue action. After years of rejecting federal support for education, Congress promptly enacted the National Defense Education Act, aimed at strengthening the schools and colleges not only in science but in foreign languages and foreign area studies. The Office of Education, suddenly turned operational by this legislation, was plunged into international educational matters on a substantial scale. How its efforts should be meshed with those of the State Department and other agencies is a problem still largely unresolved.

People to People

The Eisenhower administration, meanwhile, had been much concerned over the need for a new initiative which would dramatize the elements of popular action and private activity in international relations. The People-to-People Program, launched personally by the President in 1956, acknowledged the increased role which private individuals and organizations could play in the greatly changed postwar world. Believing that people everywhere genuinely desired peace, and acutely aware of the rigidities that often frustrate progress in government-to-government relations, President Eisenhower was anxious to mobilize and channel the good will of the American people into a massive effort to improve international understanding and friendship. The way to exploit this desire of the people for peace, he told a Washington conference of business and other leaders, was to get people together "to lead their governments—if necessary, to evade governments."

The President's challenge at first brought considerable response. Committees galore were formed and fund-raising campaigns launched to support various new programs. But this original enthusiasm waned, and the People-to-People Program eventually lapsed into obscurity (though some useful elements still remain alive with private support). In retrospect, it seems clear that the fault lay not in the President's basic assumption but in the strategy. Too little recognition was given the fact that a large and diverse people-to-people program had been under way for a long time. It included the long-standing efforts of many private organizations, working in various ways with foreign visitors and countries, sometimes in cooperation with the government. It included also the various exchange programs of the State Department which functioned in large measure through private channels and stimulated private efforts.

The need was not for still more organizations or the launching of a *new* people-to-people program, with all the fanfare and synthetic quality of an advertising campaign for some new brand. The real need was to strengthen the many existing organizations and programs which linked the private and public sectors in an authentic effort to improve international understanding. Had the same measure of presidential prestige been thrown to the support of these existing efforts, the results might have been greater and more lasting.

Late in the Eisenhower period the State Department's various exchange programs took a decided turn for the better, under the sympathetic ministrations of Secretary of State Christian Herter. Believing deeply in their importance and aware of the neglect they had suffered, he sought and secured a substantial budget increase to help regain lost ground. To unify and strengthen administration, he created a Bureau of Educational and Cultural Affairs to replace the IES, thus raising these educational activities to an administrative parity with the Department's political bureaus and providing the first step toward better internal coordination.

Herter also accepted the strong recommendation of President J. L. Morrill of the University of Minnesota, who had investigated the matter at the Department's request, that State should take the lead in coordinating all the fragmented activities of the federal government, including the technical assistance program. But Herter failed to obtain a White House mandate for this coordinating role, apparently because other agencies were not anxious to be coordinated. Robert Thayer, who headed the new Bureau, and George V. Allen, then Director of USIA, did succeed, however, in strengthening the working relationships between State and USIA. Both believed that USIA's cultural programs and officers should be returned to the State Department, but important USIA career people under Allen were less enthusiastic and the transfer never occurred.

Reorientation on the New Frontier

When President Kennedy took office in early 1961, the time was ripe and the need great to weld the government's scattered educational and cultural activities into a stronger and more coherent effort. There was no shortage of ideas about this need and how to meet it. Indeed, the new President was greeted with a number of authoritative reports with abundant recommendations on the subject.[4] Prepared by well-qualified experts, in the main private citizens, the reports reflected a strong consensus even though they approached the subject from different directions.

The common theme was that the diverse educational and cultural activities were a vitally important aspect of U.S. foreign policy and should be accorded higher priority, greater support, and stronger leadership. The reports stressed the need for clearer policy direction, better coordination, more adequate budgets, consolidation of legislation, stronger federal-private cooperation, and better collaboration within the private sector itself. Responsibility for improving the federal government's efforts, several reports urged, should be centered in a new high-level officer with clear authority to act—a new Under Secretary or Assistant Secretary of State, or a special assistant to the President.

The new administration took these recommendations seri-

---

[4] These reports are still a rich source of information and ideas. They include:

The University and World Affairs, a report by a distinguished committee sponsored by the Ford Foundation, J. L. Morrill, Chairman; John B. Howard, Study Director (New York: Ford Foundation, 1961).

Toward a National Effort in International Educational and Cultural Affairs, a report prepared for the U.S. Advisory Commission of Educational Exchange, by Walter H. C. Laves, in *Mutual Educational and Cultural Exchange Act of 1961,* Hearings before House Subcommittee on State Department Organization and Foreign Operations, 87th Cong., 1st sess., May 25–June 9, 1961 (Washington: GPO, 1961), pp. 213–294.

Report of the President's Committee on Information Activities Abroad, appointed by President Eisenhower, Mansfield Sprague, Chairman; Waldemar A. Nielsen, Executive Director. (Summarized in *Department of State Bulletin,* February 6, 1961, pp. 182–195.)

The College and University in International Affairs, in *Fifty-Fifth Annual Report of the Carnegie Foundation for the Advancement of Teaching* (New York: 1960), pp. 11–23.

Report of Task Force on "Exchange of Persons," by an *ad hoc* task force appointed by President-elect Kennedy, James M. Davis, Chairman, in *Mutual Educational and Cultural Exchange Act of 1961* (cited), pp. 295–301.

A Report to the President of the United States, transmitted by Kenneth Holland, President of the Institute for International Education.

ously. President Kennedy needed no convincing, nor did his Secretary and Under Secretary of State, Dean Rusk and Chester Bowles. All three had a deep interest and knowledge in this field. They acted promptly to create a new Assistant Secretary of State for Educational and Cultural Affairs whose assignment was, in brief, to clarify, unify, and strengthen what I have called the educational component of U.S. foreign policy.

This chapter's narrative sketch must now become an eyewitness account, since it was my lot to be chosen to fill the new post. Like any interested participant's version of a small piece of history, it must be treated with caution while awaiting the perspective of later historians when all the facts are in.

The new office quickly became a beehive of activity centering on five specific objectives, with the over-arching aim of effectively fitting educational and cultural affairs into U.S. foreign policy. They were largely organizational in nature, but behind the desire for orderly and effective procedures lay a concern with the substance of cultural relations; indeed, without a stronger organization they could not really make their proper contribution.

The first objective was to strengthen the Bureau of Educational and Cultural Affairs: welding the various units into a cohesive whole, sharpening the objectives of the exchange programs, improving their quality while simplifying procedures; above all, infusing the Bureau with fresh ideas and talent, and integrating its activities more effectively with those of other agencies. Preparation of the 1962 appropriation request became the occasion for a thoroughgoing reappraisal and replanning of the Bureau's program, built up from a fresh assessment of the needs and opportunities in each country with which we were dealing. The Bureau was then reorganized, with considerable benefit and surprisingly little pain, along geographic lines so that it could work fruitfully with the Department's "country desks" and those of USIA, and AID, and could achieve a better integration of its own programs country by country.

Another objective was to strengthen relations between government and the private sector, a process already begun under Secretary Herter. The first step, taken in the spring of 1961, was to organize nearly a dozen study groups to review critically various aspects of the whole international educational field and come up with suggestions for improvement. Some groups explored strategies for educational development in Africa, Latin America, and Asia; others focused on functional topics, such as the role of books in foreign relations or the application of new educational technologies in developing countries. Altogether, over 500 leading scholars, foundation officers, businessmen and government experts contributed. Their output of memos and reports was a rich harvest of ideas, many of which soon proved useful to government and private programs. The close working relations thus established remained fruitful long after the exercise was completed.

As an example, one field of endeavor in which government-private cooperation was particularly urgent was the selection, placement, and academic programs of the many foreign students in the United States. There were many problems and difficulties, especially for African students. Now, a series of suggested measures worked out in the new Bureau to meet those problems was widely accepted as a framework for government-private cooperation and an intensified over-all effort. And, for the first time, the federal government acknowledged a share of responsibility for those foreign students (more than 90 per cent) who came to the United States under nongovernmental auspices.

The third objective was to strengthen cooperation among various federal agencies. The essential need here was to devise clear and comprehensive guidelines by which all agencies could move more efficiently and harmoniously toward the same national goals. Talk of "coordination"—an alarming term to any bureaucrat—was avoided. It seemed more useful to seek joint solutions to specific problems where the need for coordination was conspicuously evident.

For example, when two agencies found themselves on a collision course in some foreign country—as was the case with AID and USIA in their English-teaching efforts in French-speaking Africa, and with the Peace Corps and AID in sending secondary school teachers to East Africa—it was usually possible to find a mutually acceptable solution.

The Bureau preached the gospel of "country planning" which

would mesh the activities of various agencies more rationally in relation to the major needs and special conditions of each foreign country. This planning had to be undertaken first of all in the field by those officers intimately concerned with the programs. At regional meetings USIA cultural affairs and AID education officers were brought together (for the first time) to discuss common problems and to explore ways of harmonizing their activities. Similar cooperation was initiated in Washington.

The fourth objective was to achieve greater emphasis in the various U.S. overseas programs on the development of *human* resources as a prerequisite for economic growth and social advancement in the emerging nations. It was becoming increasingly apparent that large outlays in these countries for physical facilities would be futile unless the people themselves were given new skills and knowledge to make effective use of the steel mills, modern highways, fertilizer factories, and the like. Moreover, social and political reform, urgently required in Latin America for example, would not get far without a heavy investment in education.

President Kennedy stressed this theme in his original Alliance for Progress proposal in March 1961. Educational development won a place in the Punta del Este agreements of August 1961, which spelled out the guidelines for the Alliance, and a more detailed strategy emerged from the UNESCO-OAS conference in Santiago in 1962. Elsewhere U.S. delegations also stressed the importance of education to economic growth at two other major UNESCO conferences (at Addis Ababa for African nations in 1961, and at Tokyo for Asian nations in 1962) and at the landmark Washington OECD Conference on Educational Investment and Economic Growth in late 1961.

Congress pushed in the same direction by requiring in the 1961 aid legislation that priority be given in the least developed countries to nurturing human talents as a precondition for general development. A significant advance was achieved when three major lending agencies—AID, the Inter-American Bank, and the International Development Association—reversed earlier policies and qualified educational projects for loans.

This attempt to give increased emphasis to educational development met with resistance in some quarters. Some AID economists and program officers, for example, still regarded education primarily as a social service and a consumption expenditure rather than as an investment in growth. A more serious deterrent, however, was that virtually no recipient countries had well-conceived educational development plans integrated with their economic development programs, or the personnel and institutional means to translate such plans into action. Nevertheless, encouraging progress was made, especially in getting fresh policies established, although their practical application in the field was often painfully slow and would obviously require considerable time.

The final objective was to strengthen U.S. leadership and support of international organizations dealing in educational matters, and to encourage a greater harmony of effort among them. The starting point was to improve the U.S. government's own creaky machinery for working on these questions with such organizations as UNESCO, the OECD, and the OAS. Important opportunities often fell between bureaucratic stools, and the U.S. approach was often weak, inconsistent, or confusing. As a remedy, a new "multilateral organizations" office was established in the Bureau of Educational and Cultural Affairs. The main question, of course, was what the United States would be able to do with and through the international organizations, not just what it did to improve its own institutional machinery.

It would be wrong to leave the impression that the five foregoing objectives were fully achieved in the first two years of the Kennedy administration, or even that striking progress was made. It does seem fair to say, however, that much was accomplished in tooling up for more effective and efficient future action and in generating a fresh momentum. Progress was made on clarifying the aims of various programs, reviewing and shifting basic policies, improving organizations, introducing new ideas, designing plans, and strengthening working relations within government and between government and the private sector. But an enormous job remained to be done if the educational side of U.S. foreign policy was to be developed to its full potential.

It is a fact of some interest that the foregoing objectives were pursued for many months without benefit of any executive order defining the responsibilities and authority of the new Assistant Secretary of State for Educational and Cultural Affairs. When the office was being created, Bureau of the Budget officials feared that to get such an order cleared with all the interested parties might raise many bureaucratic hackles and take too long. They were probably right. When the order finally came in mid-1962— in connection with distributing functions under the new Fulbright-Hays Act—it had to run a rugged gauntlet and emerged quite battered.

I have sometimes been asked, therefore, how it was possible without a proper driver's license to navigate Washington's cobbled bureaucratic thoroughfare with any degree of safety or success. The answer lies largely in the fact that the President himself—and such members of his official family as Vice President Lyndon Johnson, Dean Rusk, Chester Bowles, Edward R. Murrow, David Bell, Averell Harriman, Mennen Williams, Arthur Schlesinger, Jr., Sterling McMurrin, and others—were strongly convinced that the human side of U.S. foreign policy needed strengthening. They could be counted on for help, as could a number of important members of Congress, and this support set the tone. It was far more important than having an executive order with the right words.

But these top officials could not have been as helpful as they were had not many career people also been willing, indeed anxious, to improve the situation. They had lived with these programs for years, believed in them, and knew better than anyone the need for a clearer and more unified effort. The majority welcomed the opportunity to participate in a fresh effort toward this end, provided it was managed impartially and their own ideas were given a fair hearing. There were, of course, some who found it hard to see beyond the narrow confines of their own bureaucratic foxholes.

The main obstacle to getting things done in the government, I became convinced, is not the bureaucrats but the bureaucratic system itself—the entrenched rules, regulations, and procedures which victimize everyone and over which no one seems to have control. But even these man-made impediments should not be exaggerated, for it *is* possible, after all, to get a great deal done provided enough people want to see it done and someone keeps pushing.

The other great obstacle to be reckoned with, of course, is the appropriations process. If a desired action is going to cost extra money (which is by no means always the case), then it had better be viewed with some enthusiasm by members of the appropriations committees of the Congress. Even when Congress adopts overwhelmingly an excellent new piece of authorizing legislation, adequate funds must still be provided to apply the legislation effectively. The appropriations process is controlled by a small minority which can block the expressed will of a large majority of Congress. Veteran State Department officers, with heavy scar tissue from previous encounters, think twice before embracing any new action or proposal which might run afoul of the whims or prejudices of any important member of the appropriations committee. It often seems the safest course to leave well enough alone, though in fact that may be the most hazardous course for the national interest.

The Fulbright-Hays Act

A major landmark during the Kennedy administration's first year was the enactment of the Fulbright-Hays Act (by a vote of 79 to 5 in the Senate, and by 378 to 32 in the House). This measure marked a new point of maturity in America's educational and cultural relations and provided a remarkably broad, clear, and flexible framework for such relations for years to come. The Act consolidated and strengthened what had by then become a bewildering clutter of legislation. It absorbed the main elements of the original Fulbright Amendment and the Smith-Mundt Act (other than the sections of the latter on the information program) along with several lesser laws.

Among the new elements added was authority to provide services for foreign students, to establish additional centers of technical and cultural interchange such as the new "East-West Center" in Hawaii (which Vice President Johnson had earlier fathered in the Senate), to foster a "reverse flow" to the United States of foreign cultural presentations, to finance U.S.-sponsored international scholarly meetings, to collaborate with international organizations in all such activities, and to support private research on problems of educational exchange. The financial provisions were designed to free exchange programs from the bondage of foreign currency, permit the more flexible use of appropriated funds over longer periods and among agencies, and to encourage foreign governments to share in the costs of exchange activities.

Wide latitude was provided for using private organizations to administer government-sponsored programs and for broadening the functions of binational commissions overseas. The functions of the Board of Foreign Scholarships were broadened, and a new presidentially appointed U.S. Advisory Commission on International Educational and Cultural Affairs was created to serve in effect as a board of trustees for this aspect of U.S. foreign policy.

The Fulbright-Hays Act, in short, was intended to facilitate the use of virtually any and all reasonable means "to increase mutual understanding between the people of the United States and the people of other countries . . . to promote international cooperation for educational and cultural advancement; and thus to assist in the development of friendly, sympathetic, and peaceful relations between the United States and other countries of the world." As Representative Wayne Hays, who skillfully steered the measure through the House, told the Advisory Commission at its first meeting, "This law is intended to give all the possible authority needed to develop this field adequately. If you don't find what you need, ask your lawyers to look harder."

In the course of the hearings and floor debate, Senator Fulbright and Representative Hays made their positions clear on most of the perennial policy issues listed earlier in this chapter, and in approving the measure Congress implicitly endorsed these positions. "This argument . . ." Senator Fulbright said, "that the exchanges should have the primary purpose of advancing pure scholarship . . . and that any foreign policy benefits . . . should be regarded as secondary, or even incidental, I consider

. . . basically irrelevant."[5] Later he added a word on the relation of these programs to the information program. "I utterly reject any suggestion that our educational and cultural exchange programs are weapons or instruments with which to do combat. . . . There is no room, and there must not be any room, for an interpretation of these programs as propaganda, even recognizing that the term covers some very worthwhile and respectable activities."

Senator Fulbright's long-standing attitude on the latter point helps explain why, ironically, the Fulbright-Hays bill was more controversial within the Executive branch than it was in Congress. It was not, strictly speaking, an administration measure. The bill had been prepared under Senator Fulbright's direction, after consultation with many national experts, before the Kennedy administration took office. The Bureau of Educational and Cultural Affairs heartily welcomed it; other State Department officials generally approved; and AID—preoccupied at the time with drafting a new aid bill and with reorganizing itself—had no strong views. But some in the USIA who had seen the information program through many trials viewed the bill with skepticism, if not alarm. They saw in it the threat of more State Department supervision than their experience had led them to care for, and the even greater threat that USIA might be stripped of its cultural programs and cultural affairs officers. A few enthusiastic careerists in the Office of Education saw in the situation an opportunity, long desired, to secure the transfer of certain international education programs from State to their Office. As the bureaucratic winds rose, the Bureau of the Budget became conspicuously quiet and the matter soon landed in the President's lap.

It took some weeks to negotiate an agreed Executive branch position, but in the end I was authorized to testify in favor of the bill on behalf of the administration, though suggesting certain modifications. The wrangling had had its ridiculous moments and wasted valuable time, but it also had some useful lessons. Plainly the Kennedy administration had inherited in this field an accumulation of long-standing bureaucratic rivalries and

[5] *Congressional Record,* Senate, June 27, 1961, p. 10582.

anxieties which stood in the way of a unified and efficient national effort. For anyone with eyes to see, it was hard to avoid the conclusion that the time was overdue to bury the hatchets and to place national above bureaucratic interests.

The Fulbright-Hays Act greatly heartened those, in and out of government, who had worked faithfully in the vineyard of educational and cultural affairs. But in their enthusiasm many tended to forget the major hurdle that had to be jumped every year—getting adequate appropriations to implement it. For the first year after passage of the act (fiscal year 1963) the State Department was voted funds for a program only slightly larger than in the previous year. The appropriation fell far short of what seemed essential to meet the needs of foreign policy, and it dashed the high hopes raised by Congress's earlier overwhelming approval of the Fulbright-Hays Act. This was one more striking demonstration of how, in the field of educational and cultural affairs, a small number of appropriations committee members could frustrate what quite evidently had been the will of an overwhelming majority of Congress in adopting a major authorization law.

In the long run, no doubt, this law would contribute greatly to the effectiveness of U.S. foreign policy. But more than two years after its passage it still had to be ranked a relative failure in the sense that its great potential had as yet been scarcely tapped. Strengthening the educational dimension of foreign policy, though a widely heralded aim, still had a low priority on the agenda of appropriations committees and in the thinking of too many other influential people.

Chapter III

What Is Currently Going On?

Born at the onset of World War II, the educational and cultural component of U.S. foreign policy has now grown to young adulthood. Its career has been shaped by strong international and domestic pressures: a hot war followed almost immediately by a cold one, changes in national administration, new legislation, conflicting philosophies, bureaucratic rivalries. There is little wonder, then, that its purposes have often been unclear, that intelligent people have differed about its importance, and that key policy issues have never been firmly resolved.

Before considering how these issues might best be handled in the future, it will be well to look at them in their present context: at what the federal government is doing, what is happening in the private sector, and what are the educational and cultural activities of international organizations in which the United States plays an important role. These matters cannot be covered in complete detail, for no one has even inventoried all that is going on, much less arranged the scattered pieces in an orderly fashion. But for present purposes a rough thumbnail sketch will do.

Such a sketch inevitably conveys the impression of massive activity. It is a justified impression, for in truth a vast number of individuals and organizations, public and private, are engaged in a great variety of educational and cultural activities which impinge on the aims of U.S. foreign policy. One must bear in mind, however, that variety and volume of effort do not necessarily constitute adequacy. My own view, to be argued later, is that our national effort is indeed quite inadequate, both in quality and in quantity, and disorganized to the point of being chaotic. Nevertheless, it is a quite substantial one.

What the Federal Government Is Doing

Today at least two dozen federal agencies (and many more of their bureaus and subdivisions) are engaged under one label or another in international activities which fall on the educational and cultural side of foreign policy. What they are doing defies simple description. Their diverse activities, when sorted out, can be grouped roughly and somewhat arbitrarily into 43 fairly distinct categories. A glance at Appendix Tables 1 and 2 points up the extent of federal involvement.[1]

Taken in the large, such a tabular listing of activities and of the agencies concerned provides a comprehensive and accurate overview of the federal scene today, though it may not be immune to inadvertent omissions or errors of detail. It does not, of course, provide a quantitative picture. Thus two agencies engaged in the same category of activity may be doing very different amounts. One should also avoid the tempting conclusion that "wasteful duplication" exists wherever two or more agencies are listed under the same category. No doubt there is some, indeed too much. But in most instances each specialized agency is doing something for which it has a unique competence. These two caveats are illustrated by the example of the Internal Revenue Service and the Defense Department, which both provide specialized training on U.S. soil for foreign participants: the former trained 160 foreign fiscal officers in the fiscal year 1964, whereas the latter trained 15,400 foreign military personnel in the same period.[2]

The majority of agencies are, like the Internal Revenue Service, preoccupied with domestic affairs. For them, international activities are a peripheral concern, being largely centered on the

1 See pp. 144–148, below.
2 Of these 160 trainees in the Internal Revenue Service, 87 were brought to the United States for their training by some other agency, chiefly AID.

exchange of persons, the promotion of scientific and scholarly research, and participation in international organizations. By contrast, the bulk of governmental responsibilities and operations is concentrated in the five agencies primarily concerned with foreign affairs—the State Department, AID, USIA, Defense and the Peace Corps. But their work is by no means the whole story. Virtually every part of the executive branch of the federal government (and indeed the legislative and judicial branches as well) is today involved in one way or another in the educational and cultural aspects of foreign policy. Collectively their activities form a crazy-quilt pattern, which reflects the greatly enlarged international dimension of American life generally and the enormous complexity and variety of our official foreign relations. It also underscores the need for unified policy guidance and coordination of such activities if American foreign policy is to be conducted efficiently and effectively. One may appropriately ask, "Who's in charge here?"

The Department of State

The closest thing to a central switchboard in the federal government for these activities is the State Department's Bureau of Educational and Cultural Affairs (known in Washington parlance as "CU"). The Bureau now has the most inclusive charter and mission of all federal agencies in this field, the most flexible and diversified tools to work with and, potentially at least, the best vantage point from which to observe and guide the federal establishment as a whole. It does try to harmonize various governmental operations and has responsibility for coordinating U.S. policies in UNESCO and other international organizations. In reality, however, the Bureau and the Department cannot be said to be "in charge" of the array of activities carried on by all the other agencies.

CU operates a highly diversified exchange program at a cost now running over $50 million a year (including foreign currencies).[3] The largest part of it is the exchange of persons, which

---

[3] The term "exchange" in this context has come to mean any interchange of persons, ideas, and knowledge across national lines—not necessarily equal in

accounted for three-fifths of CU's budget in 1963 and involved over 10,000 individuals—roughly one-quarter American and three-quarters foreign.[4] A total of 74,210 individuals have been exchanged under State Department auspices from 1949 through 1962.

These bloodless statistics, however, do not portray the vital, human diversity involved, nor the considerable human drama. Every exchange grantee is a special case, requiring a tailor-made program. He leaves home with a particular mission in view—to study or teach, to do research, to demonstrate or advise, to observe or to work in his special field with his counterparts in another country.

This individual may be (more than half in fact are) from the academic world—a Thai girl studying English-teaching at Michigan, an Indian scholar teaching Oriental studies at a New England college, a Kenyan learning engineering at MIT, a Latin American student leader participating in an American studies seminar at Indiana. Or the foreign visitor may be a government official—a minister of education from Indonesia, a Swedish legislative leader, a promising young employee of the Colombian Planning Commission. He may be a leader in some special field—a journalist from Guinea or Ghana, the head of a Nigerian broadcasting firm, a Japanese labor leader, a Belgian artist, an Egyptian doctor, a leader of women's affairs in Togo, a Polish museum director.

The American specialists program flows in reverse. It sends talented experts abroad to work with others and to provide a deeper view of American life: a Joel Rosen, accomplished pianist and linguist, to work with music students in Latin American universities; a Ralph Magill of the *Atlanta Constitution* to Africa to render a skilled editor's honest account of race relations in

---

both directions—in which two countries cooperate. In this sense, exchanges are *bilateral* and *reciprocal*; in contrast to official information programs designed to flow in only one direction and to tell only one nation's story.

[4] A general breakdown of CU's expenditures by types of activity is shown in Appendix Table 3; a summary picture of who these people are, where they came from, and where they went is given in Appendix Table 4.

America; or a Henry Steele Commager to Italy to lecture on American life and institutions.

The Bureau also sponsors overseas tours ("cultural presentations") by outstanding American performers, with USIA handling arrangements overseas. Within present budget limits only one or two large professional or university groups can be afforded each year—such as the Boston Symphony Orchestra, the American Ballet Theatre, the University of Michigan symphonic band, the Eastman Philharmonia, or a Theatre Guild production. A larger number of individual performers and small groups are sent: an Olympic boxing or basketball team, the New York Woodwind Quintet, the Baird Marionettes, Hal Holbrook in "Mark Twain," Louis Armstrong, Isaac Stern, or Rudolf Serkin. The new authority given the State Department by the Fulbright-Hays Act to encourage a reverse flow of foreign cultural presentations to the United States through noncommercial channels has yet to be fully exercised.

CU also provides modest assistance (financial grants and exchange teachers) to private American-sponsored educational institutions serving foreign students (such as the American universities at Beirut and Cairo, Robert College in Istanbul, and Athens College) and to several dozen elementary and secondary schools that serve the children of American civilians working abroad, as well as many foreign children.

CU relies heavily upon many cooperating agencies to help administer its programs, including the binational "Fulbright Commissions" overseas, several private nonprofit agencies in the United States such as the Conference Board of Associated Research Councils, the Governmental Affairs Institute, and the Institute of International Education, and such federal agencies as the U.S. Office of Education and the Department of Labor.

In cooperation with the Bureau of International Organizations, CU also exercises responsibility for developing U.S. policies and programs relating to the educational and cultural activities of such multilateral agencies as UNESCO, the Organization of American States, and the Organization for Economic Cooperation and Development.

The United States Information Agency

USIA's mission, in the words of its former Director, Edward R. Murrow, is "to further the achievement of US foreign policy objectives . . . by influencing public attitudes abroad in support of these objectives . . . through personal contact, radio broadcasting, libraries, television, exhibits, English language instruction, and others."[5]

It would be incorrect to interpret the words "influencing public attitudes abroad" as implying a propaganda function in the narrow and invidious sense. When he took office in 1961, Murrow declared that "truth is the best propaganda" for the United States and that USIA would stick to the truth, even when it hurt. His basic aim, he made clear repeatedly, was to convey to others an accurate and sympathetic understanding of American life and policies, and to destroy mischievous misconceptions nurtured by others. This is a task with both long-run and short-run dimensions, to be pursued not only through news programs and "fast media" but through a variety of wider-range educational and cultural means.

Viewed in these terms, USIA obviously has much in common with CU, as both are engaged in promoting honest understanding. A major difference, however, is that USIA is confined by its legislation to working on only one side of the equation of understanding—the understanding of the United States by others—whereas CU works both sides.

The lion's share of USIA's budget is committed to current information activities and the explanation of official U.S. policies, yet more than is generally realized goes into basic educational and cultural activities. Over one-fifth of the fiscal 1964 operating budget of $145.8 million went into overseas programs of books and libraries, English-teaching, and various exhibits of American life. USIA estimates that more than half of its Voice of America broadcasts, TV programs, films, and publications is devoted to

5 Statement by Edward R. Murrow before the Sub-Committee on International Organizations and Movements of the House Committee on Foreign Affairs, March 28, 1963.

essentially educational and cultural content having no direct bearing on political affairs and current events. USIA has 205 cultural and educational officers overseas to handle both its own activities and the State Department's exchange program.

Books play a central role in USIA's cultural program. Its 316 well stocked libraries, reading rooms, and binational cultural centers served 30 million foreign users in 1964. The standard collection (wholly American in origin though including foreign translations when available) includes an excellent assortment of basic reference works, U.S. government documents, biography and fiction, professional and technical journals, and popular periodicals. With their "information please" service, these libraries have become influential local research centers. They are used by professors, students, lawyers, engineers, public officials, and ordinary citizens in search of ideas and information on everything from airplane engines to constitutional law. USIA also assists the production and sale of American books through commercial channels at moderate prices, both in English and in translation; supports local production of low-cost textbooks with U.S.-owned foreign currencies; makes gifts of American books and magazines to local educational institutions and key foreign leaders; and helps American publishers to market their books in countries where currency exchange difficulties exist.

The most booming item in USIA's catalogue, however, is the English language itself, for which the foreign demand can only be called insatiable. In the last 10 years, more than 1,600,000 people have had classroom instruction in English at partially self-supporting binational cultural centers, many of them important local functionaries who need English for very practical purposes. The Agency's new TV series for English instruction was on the air from 59 stations in 37 countries in fiscal 1964.

As in the case of CU, the recitation of these various USIA activities and statistics leaves an impression of large and far-reaching activity, which in one sense is correct. But when measured against the world-wide opportunities and demand—for example, for reading American books and for learning English— the actual scale of effort is exceedingly modest.

The Agency for International Development (AID)

Fowler Hamilton, first AID Director under President Kennedy, was fond of saying that AID was above all else "in the business of education, with a small *e*." To him education with a big "E" meant formal schooling (in which AID is also involved), but with the lower-case letter it meant all kinds of useful learning, in and out of school, including that imparted through technical assistance. Like many others, Hamilton had become convinced that the acquisition of new knowledge and skills by the peoples of developing countries was an indispensable requirement for modernizing these countries. His successor, David Bell, needed no convincing; he had in fact spent some years putting the principle into practice in Pakistan, under a Harvard project financed by the Ford Foundation.

AID and its predecessor agencies have certainly been much involved in education, whether of the formal or informal type. The difficulty is in trying to find out just how much it has been involved. AID's reporting system is better designed to serve the needs of congressional examiners, who want to know whether the money was honestly spent, than the needs of others who want to know what it was spent for; and, unfortunately, no adequate record is available on how large a role education has played in the U.S. aid program. Clearly it has been small relative to the total program, for the funds have largely gone into capital projects and general budgetary support, but a few salient figures will demonstrate that education is, nevertheless, a factor of some significance. In fiscal year 1963 AID brought nearly 5,800 trainees from developing nations to the United States and sent over 2,120 more for specialized training and education in other countries. In the same year AID obligated, for expenditures over a period of years, about $181 million for educational projects (e.g., support to local institutions of higher education, teacher-training institutions, vocational schools and the like).[6] As of the spring of 1964 the Agency had some 300 educational advisers overseas and contracts with 71 American universities to help carry out its educa-

[6] This includes $62.8 million in dollar development grants plus $118.2 million in PL 480 funds.

tional projects. Relatively few AID loans for educational projects had yet been made, however, despite the policy decision to go ahead with them.

AID, like CU, also brings leaders and specialists (as distinct from trainees) from developing countries for short visits to the United States. But except for using the same "reception centers," administered by the State Department, these two flows are handled independently, sometimes to the embarrassment of the U.S. government.

The Peace Corps

The Peace Corps, the most exciting venture of all at the moment, has thus far made an enviable record. At the end of 1963, it had almost 7,000 volunteers in 46 countries and was expected to have some 10,000 in the field by the end of 1964. A large number were serving as teachers of English and other subjects, and their success in the secondary schools prompted the Peace Corps to consider helping faculty-hungry foreign universities. Other volunteers, serving on health projects, highway survey teams, and the like, were also much engaged in teaching (and learning a good deal in the process).

What the Peace Corps is actually accomplishing in the countries where its members are at work cannot be judged as yet. It gives promise of making a real contribution to foreign policy objectives even without any conscious connection with them, and perhaps largely for that reason. At home, there is already an avid demand by government, educational institutions, and others for Peace Corps veterans who started returning home by mid-1963, after two years overseas. It was widely agreed that their experience abroad had provided valuable new resources for the conduct of our foreign relations.

The Department of Defense

One does not usually think of the military services as being involved in educational and cultural affairs, yet in several respects they do the most. Each year, for example, Defense brings more foreign trainees to the United States than AID and the State Department combined. Some of these trainees, as the headlines repeatedly show, later reach high political office back home (on occasion by force, though their specialized U.S. military training was meant for a quite different purpose).

The military services give extensive support to scientific research in foreign universities and other institutions, much of it basic research not tied to military applications. They teach English to approximately 25,000 foreigners a year, largely military personnel. Their broadcasting network around the world with over 200 radio and 38 TV transmitters, is larger than that of the USIA. The armed service broadcasts are intended for our own servicemen, and the program content is often not what USIA experts would regard as ideal for foreign audiences. But in fact the "bootleg" foreign audience of the armed services network is larger than that reached by the Voice of America and is believed to outnumber overseas American listeners by about twenty to one.

The ubiquitous presence of the American military around the world inevitably affects American cultural and political relations, sometimes beneficially, other times not. The military services have made a large effort to build assets and minimize liabilities in this respect, but obviously no amount of "orientation" and "community relations programs" can guarantee uniformly favorable results. One positive result, often overlooked, is the extensive knowledge of other societies which many officers and servicemen acquire overseas, particularly those working in developing countries. Unfortunately, the system of military reassignment often wastes this rich experience. To their credit, the military services (with more abundant funds for the purpose) are doing a better job than most civilian agencies in providing intensive training for their foreign area specialists, including sending them to major university centers.

Federal "Domestic" Agencies

We turn briefly to the federal agencies which are primarily concerned with domestic affairs. Those which contribute usefully to international affairs are usually specialized in one or another field such as health, map-making, road-building, mining, or agriculture. They are uniquely equipped to receive and train visiting foreign specialists in their field, to tap specialized knowledge and manpower for international use in the AID program or otherwise to represent the U.S. government and scientific community at professional meetings, and to confer and collaborate with their counterparts overseas.

The Office of Education, to take an example, handles many visiting foreign educators, arranges exchanges of foreign and American school teachers for the State Department, makes studies of foreign educational systems, and helps recruit education specialists for AID. Under the National Defense Education Act, it also provides assistance to American schools, colleges and universities to improve teaching and research in foreign languages and area study.

Where the money comes from to support all these international activities of the domestic agencies, and how much is involved, are often moot questions. The federal government has no "international" budget, much less a budget for the educational and cultural part of foreign policy. Many of these costs are tucked away in individual agency budgets, often under the most unlikely rubrics. Nor, in most cases, would one find explicit legislative authorization for the international activities of these agencies. The tide of international involvement has swept too fast to permit suitable legislative and budget arrangements. And no doubt many agencies, anxious to maintain their international dimension, have not wished to raise the issue with Congress, lest they be told to discontinue their foreign activities.

What the Private Sector Is Doing

Despite the considerable international activities of federal agencies, there could scarcely be an educational component of U.S. foreign policy were it not for the willingness of private agencies and individuals to cooperate. The private sector—individuals, the academic community, voluntary organizations, foundations, and private business—contributes in two distinct ways. One way is to assist directly, usually under contract and for payment, in carrying out particular government programs or projects through private channels. In such cases the government has a major voice and the private agency is, in a sense, an instrument of government policy. But even here the private agency usually insists upon and is given considerable latitude, or else refuses the contract.

On a far broader scale, however, private agencies and individuals independently pursue educational and cultural activities which shape foreign relations and impinge, often quite unintentionally, on foreign policy. The vast sprawl of private endeavors cannot be readily measured, but clearly it exceeds the total of direct official programs. Government's role predominates only in those situations where voluntary private efforts cannot be expected to fill important specific needs of national interest, such as running overseas libraries, supporting scientific research in particular countries, providing technical assistance to developing nations, or conducting certain types of exchange programs.

Some important national needs, however, can only be met by voluntary private efforts, such as providing good instruction, guidance, and hospitality to foreign students. Public funds may be available, but unless universities and other institutions can and will do the job, the government is relatively powerless and the national interest suffers.

In other cases private actions (and "private foreign policies," as it were) may collide with the national interest—as when private companies export the sorts of books, films and TV programs or pursue certain overseas investment and management practices, which threaten to impair relations with other nations and perhaps defeat the government's own efforts. Here again the government is largely powerless to act, beyond presenting its case and appealing for private cooperation.

In short, despite what the Constitution says, the federal government does not alone conduct U.S. foreign relations. Acting on their own, private citizens and organizations have a great deal to do with it.

Individuals

America's cultural relations with the world are carried on daily, often quite unwittingly, by all kinds of individuals who come into contact with foreigners abroad or at home—tourists, students, missionaries, journalists, novelists, actors and producers, soldiers and sailors, businessmen, technical experts, even American families doing their bit for international understanding by serving dinner to foreign students. In a recent year there were about one and one-half million Americans living abroad— some just living, some working on their own, and about 100,000 working for one or another American organization. Of the latter, according to Harlan Cleveland and his collaborators in *The Overseas Americans*,[7] about one-third were government employees, one-quarter businessmen, and just under one-third missionaries. What they were doing, these investigators concluded, was "involving themselves in the internal affairs of other nations." The manner in which the massive influence of the United States is brought to bear "depends mostly on the individual Americans who carry power into action around the globe."

What an individual on his own can contribute to good foreign relations is sometimes astonishing. Our able Ambassador to Mali wrote to me in 1962 about such a case.

A young American . . . is leaving Mali tomorrow after having spent an academic year as a teacher of English in a town . . . of about 7,000. . . . An anthropology major, he decided after graduation to spend a year in Mali—knocked on the door of the Ministry of Education asking whether there was need for an English teacher. They snapped him up immediately and put him to work. I don't think that he has regretted a moment of the past nine months nor do I think the town will forget him.

Here was an example of an American dealing directly with a foreign government and offering his services at a bargain rate and giving his best in return. We need more of this sort of thing. . . . I doubt that there is anything that has produced more good will to the United States in the past year in Mali than the work done by this young fellow, and it did not cost us a penny.

[7] New York: McGraw-Hill, 1960.

This may seem an exceptional case, but in a large sense it is not. Every day hundreds of Americans, at home and abroad, go out of their way to render useful service to foreigners or to have a fruitful interchange. Their reward is new knowledge and insight, and a warm sense of having contributed something worthwhile.

The Educational Community

The great changes in the world and in the nation's intertional involvements over the past two decades have imposed a heavy new set of tasks upon American educational institutions. They must, for one thing, prepare today's young Americans to live in a very different world as citizens, specialists, and leaders. This requires modifying the curriculum in many ways and broadening it beyond its earlier almost exclusive preoccupation with the Western world. It means training and retraining teachers in international subjects, strengthening research and instruction in foreign areas and languages. Our universities are now called on to uncover new knowledge needed to strengthen the nation's capacity to act wisely and effectively in world affairs and to prepare competent experts to carry out new and important international tasks. They also have an obligation to broaden and deepen, through various channels of adult learning, the older generation's perceptions of the world.

On top of these "domestic" requirements, American colleges and universities (private and tax-supported alike) have a large new set of foreign clients—individual students and whole nations. Foreign students are coming to American campuses in even greater numbers. Some 64,000 were here in the 1962–63 academic year,[8] and the total is rising by over 10 per cent annually. And now these campuses reach across the world to serve foreign clients where they live—in Chile and Colombia, Korea and India, Nigeria and Kenya.

American schools, colleges, and universities have made impressive progress in adjusting to these new tasks, but much further progress is needed. Meanwhile the available resources are strained. Foreign students, for example, are a major expense to

[8] *Open Doors 1963*, a report by the Institute of International Education.

many colleges and universities. Fewer than 10 per cent receive any help through federal exchange programs, and even then each government dollar must typically be matched by two to four dollars from another source (which in practice usually means the colleges and universities). The other 90 per cent of foreign students impose an even heavier burden upon educational institutions, whose total outlays for such purposes considerably exceed the federal government's.

In short, American education is being revolutionized in response to the same changes that are affecting American foreign policy and the world itself. And well it should be, for it constitutes in the long haul the nation's chief means for adjusting successfully to a vastly altered world. Tomorrow's makers of foreign policy are being taught in today's schools.

Voluntary Organizations

Also active in foreign affairs is a vast array of professional, cultural, civic and religious organizations. Some collaborate directly with government agencies; many work with the U.S. National Commission for UNESCO; but most go their separate ways, with aims that may vary from peace and international understanding to the encouragement of trade or the spread of Esperanto, or merely the enlightenment of their members. Some of their activities, abroad or at home, may be more hindrance than help to those responsible for the conduct of U.S. foreign policy. But by and large, through the great diversity of their interests they strengthen the basis for what still has to be developed, an effective educational component of U.S. foreign policy.

Some organizations specialize in foreign affairs, fostering research, informing Americans, handling foreign visitors, managing international exchanges. Illustrative of these are the Foreign Policy Association and its numerous community affiliates, the Institute of International Education, the Council on Student Travel, the African-American Institute, the National Association of Foreign Student Advisers. Then there are the professional societies, like the numerous affiliates of the American Council of Learned Societies, the National Research Council, the Social

Science Research Council, and the American Bar Association, again to name but a few. Such organizations have helped place the nation's specialized talent at the disposal of both our own government and other nations. They have sponsored important international studies and activities and have contributed in numerous other ways.

Private cultural institutions also play an important role. A notable example is the International Council of the Museum of Modern Art which, with other museums and galleries and a few hundred private collectors, has sent more than 100 substantial exhibitions of American graphic arts to about 60 foreign countries. One of these, The Family of Man, had a foreign audience exceeding 9 million. Recently the Council has emphasized exhibits of design and architecture which combine aesthetic quality and practical utility on topics of special interest to developing nations, such as city planning and the construction of schools, hospitals, airports and factories. Through its traveling exhibits, its "art in embassies" project, the presentation of books and visual materials to foreign institutions, and its exchanges of specialists, the Council has done much which government alone cannot do to acquaint the rest of the world with the artistic accomplishments of the United States.

The largest and most diversified group of all are the civic, fraternal, religious, and occupational groups that run the gamut of American life: women voters and women professionals; farmers young and old; Catholics, Protestants and Jews; labor and business; friends of museums, orchestras and books; Americans with an interest in Japan or the Middle East, Africa or Latin America. Hundreds of such organizations have lately acquired a new international interest or expanded an old one by such means as organizing foreign affairs study groups, entertaining foreign visitors, supporting overseas educational and other projects, sending emissaries abroad, and financing international fellowships. This widespread activity reflects the greater awareness of most Americans of how important it is to know more about the world and work on friendly terms with people of other nations. One-sided and ill-informed as some of it has been, on the whole it has also helped create a more enlightened climate of public opinion in support of crucial foreign policies and programs.

Private Foundations

Several of the major private foundations have been influential pace setters in the educational and cultural realm of U.S. foreign relations. The Rockefeller philanthropies were running flourishing Point Four types of programs in Latin America and elsewhere long before President Truman introduced the term. They have continued to practice creative philanthropy around the world, especially in agricultural, medical and cultural affairs, and lessons they learned earlier have served other foundations and the government well.

The Carnegie Corporation also has a distinguished history of international philanthropy, particularly in the British Commonwealth nations and territories. Recently it has been playing a highly imaginative catalytic role to strengthen and mobilize American education to meet international requirements and to help fashion new strategies for educational development in the modernizing countries.

The Carnegie Endowment for International Peace, which Andrew Carnegie once seriously thought would have worked itself out of a job before now, continues to contribute importantly to the search for peaceful solutions to the world's ills and especially for ways to strengthen the U.N. system.

Several smaller and less-known foundations are having an important impact in selected ways. Phelps-Stokes has for many years supported useful work on African affairs; Kellogg is expanding its support of international education; Hazen is giving imaginative support to intercultural understanding, particularly between the Orient and Occident, and is currently supporting an independent study on the role of U.S. cultural affairs officers.

The fat boy in the philanthropic canoe—as Dean Rusk once dubbed the Ford Foundation—began paddling hard only in 1950 but soon became the world's largest private philanthropic force. By late 1961, out of total Ford grants of $1.5 billion, more than 20 per cent ($446 million, to be exact) had gone into world affairs. Much of this went into American education, mainly for study and research on foreign areas and languages by American scholars, to boost our own competence. Some money was directed at strengthening the Atlantic community, for example, through support of multinational institutes and cultural interchange. Some grants also helped open an intellectual dialogue with Communist scholars and eased the way for later government programs of this sort. But the largest share of Ford's "world affairs" money has gone into technical assistance and institution-building in some forty countries of Asia, Africa, and Latin America, with heavy emphasis on education.

Through strategic demonstration projects at home and abroad in foreign area studies, language teaching, community development, and other fields, these foundations have many times given light and guidance to governments all over the world, including our own. The fresh models initiated and tested by them have set patterns for much larger governmental efforts. These philanthropies jealously guard their independence of government, yet their actions have unquestionably contributed much to the advancement of the underlying purposes of U.S. foreign policy.

Private Business

All through history commercial relations have been accompanied by important cultural influences, and now the pace has quickened. American business—in the early 1960s accounting for about 13 per cent of the world's total imports, 18 per cent of exports, and nearly 40 per cent of the long-term private capital flow from advanced Western nations to developing countries—is inescapably playing a major role in cultural relations.

Some American business firms operating today in less developed countries more closely resemble private Point Four programs than the old image of hard-boiled capitalists "exploiting the natives." The more experienced and enlightened companies know full well that to be successful and to be allowed to stay in a foreign country they must put down firm roots, develop a competent and healthy labor force, advance local citizens to positions of responsibility, and above all respect the needs, aspirations, and rights of local people. To meet these practical necessities, companies have initiated educational, training, and social welfare programs in foreign countries on an impressive scale. In so doing they have become a profoundly revolutionary force, often to the discomfort of less progressive local entrepreneurs. This, of course, is not the universal rule. There are still embarrassing exceptions, but their number is declining.

American exporters in the communications field are unquestionably doing more to shape the average foreigner's "image" of the United States than is the USIA, and sometimes in contrary directions. American publishers, for example, send far more books abroad than the U.S. government—about $100 millions' worth in 1962. Many represent this nation's finest literary and technical accomplishments, but an uncomfortably large proportion, one ruefully discovers in visiting foreign shops, are of the slick and sleazy type which are all too evident at home.

American movies, some foreign observers believe, are the strongest single force shaping foreign impressions of American life. Each week about 150 million non-Americans around the world view the best and the worst that Hollywood has to offer. When asked in a 1962 congressional hearing whether he agreed that exported American films "were all good and making a great impact for the United States," Edward R. Murrow replied: "I would not agree that they are all good; no sir. We [USIA] made . . . a wholly informal, unscientific study of the impact of U.S. movies abroad . . . the conclusion was that on balance, by a rather narrow margin, they helped us more than they hurt; but it also reflected that some movies do us very considerable damage abroad, sir."[9]

Rapidly expanding exports of television programs, now more than $60 million a year, are rivaling the movies as a shaper of foreign conceptions, and misconceptions, of American society. In many countries of Latin America, Asia, and Africa more than half the television fare is "made in U.S.A." In Cairo I learned in 1961 that the Egyptians "love Lucy" best of all. Tokyo depart-

[9] Departments of State, Justice and Commerce, the Judiciary and Related Agencies Appropriations for 1963; Hearings, House of Representatives, 87th Cong., 2d sess., March 14, 1962 (Washington: GPO, 1962), p. 35.

ment stores, I was assured in 1962, were outdoing the earlier U.S. retail boom in Hopalong Cassidy suits and sidearms for children, thanks to American TV Westerns. A Nigerian TV fan asked a visiting interviewer some time ago, "When are you people going to get cars like us? All you seem to ride is horses." Westerns can be dismissed as harmless fun, but some observers are deeply disturbed by exports of tapes featuring crime, delinquency, and other sordid subjects that may reflect one aspect of our society but are hardly representative of American life as a whole. Private exporters reply by pointing to the increase in public service and cultural programs and good quality documentaries being shipped abroad which hopefully will improve the blend.

Here at home American business is playing a constructive role in extending hospitality, special services, and training opportunities to foreign visitors, including labor leaders from many countries and technicians from the Soviet Union and Eastern Europe. The latter are frequently surprised to discover that American capitalists do not fit the Marxist caricature.

With its philanthropies American industry is becoming more active in international educational and cultural affairs, though the total scale is still very modest. The American-backed Creole Foundation in Venezuela, for example, has a distinguished record of fellowship aid to Latin American youth, as does Ford Motor Company which supports rural youth clubs there. The Heinz Company and Johnson Wax Company have financed overseas tours of American musical performances and art. Pittsburgh Plate Glass recently started a special fellowship program in the United States for advanced foreign students.

What International Agencies Are Doing

To complete the sketch, account must be taken of U.S.-supported international organizations which are engaged in a wide variety of educational, cultural, scientific and technical assistance activities. The number is astonishing, almost forty.[10] They vary greatly in size; most specialize in a particular field such as health

10 Appendix Table 5 lists these international organizations, with a general indication of what they do.

or education or labor; many are within the U.N. system, while others are regional bodies unaffiliated with the U.N.

Such agencies cannot, of course, be regarded as instruments of U.S. foreign policy because many other nations also have a voice in running them. Yet, by helping developing countries to modernize themselves and consolidate their independence and by strengthening international cooperation at a very practical level, they can and do reinforce important objectives of our foreign policy, often in ways not available to the U.S. government itself.

Substantially the most important in educational and cultural affairs is UNESCO, the United Nations Educational, Scientific and Cultural Organization, which is involved in a remarkable variety of world-wide activities.[11] Under the pressure of member countries and various specialized groups, UNESCO at one time or another has been involved in almost everything one can imagine that deals with the life of the mind—books and libraries, the writing of history, the preservation of ancient monuments, fellowships, art, the International Geophysical Year, mass communication—to name only some of its concerns covering education, science, and culture in the broadest sense.

Anyone encountering this range of activities around the world would assume that UNESCO is huge and well financed. Quite the contrary is the case. Its regular budget is about $20 million a year (a scant third the size of that of the State Department's Bureau of Educational and Cultural Affairs and one-sixth that of USIA). It also administers for the U.N. Special Fund and the U.N. Technical Assistance program about the same amount of funds for educational projects. Currently the U.S. government's assessed contribution to UNESCO is about $6 million a year. But the importance of UNESCO is to be judged less by how much it spends than by what it does that others cannot do and by its demonstrated capacity for mobilizing human and other resources.

[11] An excellent brief analysis of what this unique organization does, and of U.S. policy toward it, is provided in a recent book by George N. Shuster (who was there at UNESCO's birth in 1946 and has helped nurture it through the years) entitled *UNESCO: Assessment and Promise* (New York: Harper & Row, 1963), in the Council on Foreign Relations Policy Book series.

UNESCO has two particularly strategic assets: the expertise and international leadership position it has developed, especially in educational planning and development, and the great confidence it enjoys among the emerging nations. These countries understandably prefer to get advice on the politically delicate matter of shaping their educational future from an international agency they consider objective rather than from an individual nation with a possible axe to grind. Thus UNESCO has lately been overwhelmed with requests for educational planning assistance from its less developed members, and with requests for professional and administrative cooperation on educational development from other international agencies such as the U.N. Special Fund, the U.N. Expanded Technical Assistance Board, the World Bank, and the Inter-American Development Bank. Under these pressures UNESCO has become a much more operational agency than it was originally designed to be. Hence it is now having to go through the painful business of reorganizing itself to handle this new pattern of activities more effectively, trying at the same time to reduce the excessive scattering of its program.

To bolster world-wide educational development, UNESCO established an International Institute for Educational Planning in Paris in 1963, with help from the World Bank, the Ford Foundation, and the French government. The new institute's basic mission is to help, through advanced training and research, to expand the supply of useful knowledge and of qualified experts in this field, and to encourage a better integration of education with over-all economic and social development.

Perhaps as important as what UNESCO does is the spirit in which it is done. Since the club belongs to rich and poor alike, there is far less a drawing of lines between giver and receiver than in bilateral programs. And even people from hostile ideological camps often find their differences submerged in cooperative endeavors under UNESCO's banner. Other U.N. organizations that have some of those same advantages are the International Labor Organization, the World Health Organization, the Food and Agriculture Organization, and the Children's Fund, all of which are doing significant work in developing and applying human skills and knowledge in their respective fields.

Illustrative of the regional organizations outside the U.N. system are the Organization for Economic Cooperation and Development and its Development Assistance Committee, through which the United States, Canada, and Western European countries have pioneered in the use of scientific and technical manpower and the relationship of educational investment to economic growth. Another is the Organization of American States, which has acquired heavy responsibilities for educational and cultural leadership under the Alliance for Progress, recently exercised, for example, by its Task Force on Education that undertook to chart an educational development strategy for all Latin America.

Regular U.S. government contributions to all these international organizations totaled just over $40 million in 1963 (not counting $27 million to the United Nations itself). A substantial fraction—no one knows just how much—goes into educational and cultural activities, most of which are not only compatible with but decidedly helpful to the broad objectives of American foreign policy. Its contributions through these international agencies, of course, are only a tiny fraction of the funds which the United States spends for similar purposes through bilateral channels. The same being true for other major powers, it can safely be concluded that educational and cultural relations the world over are still conducted largely on a bilateral basis and shaped according to each nation's own interests as it sees them. Unless and until the work of the international organizations is greatly expanded, this is the main framework within which our achievements must be judged and our policies developed.

Chapter IV

What Are Other
Nations Doing?

The two preceding chapters examined the growth and current state of American foreign policy's educational component, and the next chapter will assess its accomplishments, shortcomings, and potentialities. Any such assessment must take account also of the strategies and actions of other nations which complement or compete with U.S. efforts in this field.

The extent of other national efforts is clearly substantial, though unfortunately there exists no good comparative analysis of them. A survey by UNESCO in 1959 revealed that well over half of the 81 member states queried, including virtually all the larger ones, had official cultural relations programs. The number of countries and the scale of their activities are undoubtedly even larger today. Since limitations of space and evidence rule out a more comprehensive review, this chapter provides a tiny sketch of the cultural relations background and current policies and programs of four major European powers, France, the United Kingdom, Germany, and the Soviet Union.[1]

[1] I am indebted to several officials of the first three of these nations for supplying me with current information and for making valuable comments on an earlier draft of this chapter. For data on recent Soviet activities I have relied mainly upon unclassified U.S. government reports and on Frederick Barghoorn's *The Soviet Cultural Offensive* (Princeton: University Press, 1960). The historical references have been drawn primarily from Ruth McMurry and Muna Lee, *The Cultural Approach—Another Way in International Relations* (Chapel Hill: University of North Carolina Press, 1947).

France: Conquest by Spirit

France has made cultural relations a serious element of its foreign policy ever since Napoleon's Egyptian campaign and has had no equal in the field. Today, more than half the Foreign Ministry's budget is devoted to cultural activities, and the overseas aid program puts its heaviest emphasis on education. "France believes," a recent official report states, "that the human factor is paramount in the accelerated economic development of these overseas countries. For the individual represents both the end and the means."[2]

A few facts bear testimony to the seriousness of the French effort in this field:

The French government spent more than $100 million in 1962 on education in developing countries, primarily in Africa and Southeast Asia.

Over 30,000 French teachers, regular members of the national educational establishment, were serving abroad in 1963—the great majority in former French territories of Africa and Southeast Asia, but over 250 in Latin America. At least an equal number of other French citizens, many of them members of religious orders, were also teaching abroad. This vastly exceeds the total of American and British teachers overseas.

About 10,000 French technical assistance experts were stationed overseas under government auspices in 1961, engaged chiefly in "on-the-spot training of middle management, skilled labor and other qualified personnel." (The nearest comparable figure for AID was 1,190.)

Some 30,000 foreign students were studying in French universities in 1963, more than 20,000 of them from developing countries. Over 10,000 Africans were attending French universities, engineering schools, and business schools in 1961—several times the number of Africans studying in the United States that year. In addition to special scholarships for some, the French government provides all foreign students free tuition, subsidized meals, social security services, and other advantages enjoyed by French students. (This assistance, incidentally, makes it financially possible for many American students to spend a year of study in France.)

2 *France—Aid and Cooperation,* published by the Service de Presse et d'Information of the French Embassy, Washington, D.C., 1963, p. 3.

Approximately 3,000 foreign technicians come to France under government auspices each year for specialized training in French Government offices or businesses and in special schools—about half from Africa, one-quarter from Latin America, and over 10 per cent from Asia.

The Ministry of Foreign Affairs supports about one hundred French libraries overseas. Twice this number are run by the Alliance Française, a private cultural organization encouraged by the government. In addition, about one hundred overseas phonograph record centers and a similar number of film libraries are supported by the government. Book gifts totaling $200,000 were made in 1961.

In a recent year the Foreign Ministry supported sixty tours of theater groups to thirty-eight different countries; seventy-seven tours by musicians (symphonies, chamber music ensembles and individual virtuosos); and about twenty art exhibits.

The Alliance Française runs about 800 cultural centers outside France for teaching the French language and civilization. (In the United States, however, the Alliances Françaises are independent American groups, not administratively connected with Paris, and are usually more social than instructional.)

These substantial current efforts are in keeping with a policy of long standing, about which the French have never minced words and in whose efficacy they have great confidence. The theme was sounded by Napoleon in his twilight reflections at St. Helena: "I have been forced to conquer Europe by the sword; he who comes after will conquer it by the spirit. For the spirit is always more powerful than the sword." For Napoleon, and for French leaders after him, this was not a matter of nostalgia or sentiment but of hard realism. "Intellectual and moral expansion," as the French called it, was aimed at the elites of other societies and became a major instrument in building and assimilating the second great French colonial empire of the late nineteenth century. Wherever possible, cultural penetration was substituted for force. "What political operation or armed invasion," a French deputy candidly asked his colleagues in 1900, "was ever able, with less expense, to produce such important and lasting results?"

French universities and French overseas schools were called "true centers of propaganda in favor of France" by an official report in 1920 which asserted that "the Ministry of Foreign

Affairs and its agents abroad must direct and control efforts, inspire and encourage at any price French intellectual penetration, in the conviction that it is one of the surest and most effective of our activities abroad—one of our foreign policies that is richest in resources and least debatable." Although French cultural relations programs have been administered separately from economic and information programs, their commercial and political advantages have not been ignored. The view expressed by a French deputy in 1912 is still alive today: "If commerce follows the flag, it follows for even stronger reasons the national language."

With the liquidation of the colonial empire after World War II, France has redoubled its cultural effort, shifting the strategy from the promotion of what was earlier called "assimilation" to what is now called "contractual cooperation" with the former colonies and territories. This, again, is much more than a sentimental affair, though the sentiments run deep on both sides. It is part of a strategic effort to consolidate a large, close-knit, French-speaking cultural and economic community—somewhat comparable to the British Commonwealth—that will fortify the political and economic position of France and sustain its international power and prestige.

It is plain that these old French cultural ties are made of strong fiber—rugged enough, for example, to have survived the angry Bizerte incident in Tunisia in 1961. Though political relations at that time reached the breaking point, educational and cultural cooperation remained in full force.

Building on past accomplishments, France seems well on the way to consolidating a "culture empire"—based now on voluntary membership—which may well prove more viable and profitable than its two lost political empires. It could prove an asset also to the whole democratic world by helping to insure the independence, prosperity, and stability of the twenty or so new nations of Africa and Asia that have now emerged where the second French Empire once stood. But all this, one suspects, will hinge partly on whether the French have the foresight to permit and indeed to encourage these new nations to build supplemental cultural ties with other advanced democratic nations too, for without that they can scarcely feel fully independent.

There is also the question whether France's cultural effort will become more broadly international both geographically and psychologically. The impressively large educational aid effort, for example, is largely confined to the former French territories in Africa, whereas aid to Latin American countries, which would undoubtedly welcome more, is very modest. In part this concentration reflects a conspicuous need to make up for lost time in building indigenous educational systems staffed by Africans. But it also reflects—on the part of some French officials, though by no means all—the survival of a narrow nationalistic approach to cultural relations. Others argue that this high concentration represents a failure to grasp the opportunity and obligation to bring France's great cultural and economic strengths to bear on the larger, cooperative task of harmonizing the entire community of independent nations, old and new alike. The future course of French cultural relations will be strongly affected by the outcome of this current debate within France between defenders of a narrow nationalism and proponents of a broader international view.

The United Kingdom: National Interpretation

British experience is especially rich in possible lessons for the United States. The approaches of both nations are philosophically close and, being relatively new in the field, both are less inhibited by tradition from striking out in fresh directions. The British, like the Americans, were initially pushed into an offical cultural relations program by the hostile maneuvers of nazism and fascism, but once in, they rather liked it. They approached the matter in a uniquely English fashion, mainly through the British Council—one of those private arms of government which non-Britishers find hard to fathom.

Working for years on a shoestring, the Council did an impressive job, and its activities have grown far beyond the original vision. For its size, the British cultural relations program is perhaps unequalled in quality and effectiveness, though some critics consider it too stuffy and unimaginative. To judge from the greater budgetary support now provided, Her Majesty's Government is convinced, even if tardily as history goes, that educational and cultural affairs deserve an important role in foreign policy.

The British Council's central mission from the start was described as "national interpretation," which was regarded as "a happier phrase than cultural propaganda." To avoid any suspicion of propaganda, even in wartime, the Council's management has been kept in distinguished private hands and sharply divorced from the British Information Service. While substantially autonomous and semi-private in character, the Council receives most of its funds from Parliamentary grants and cooperates closely with the Foreign Office. Its budget rose from about £3 million in 1953 to £8 million in 1963, not counting substantial technical assistance funds which the Council administers for other national and international bodies.

The British program (like the American) is notably broader geographically than either the French or German, despite a heavy concern for former colonies and the Commonwealth. Well over half the Council's 1963 "Regional Services" budget was earmarked for countries outside the Commonwealth. Its overseas offices serve some seventy-five countries and territories. While the Council's earlier emphasis on teaching English and disseminating British books and other publications still continues, important new activities have now been added, including extensive work with foreign students and other visitors, sending British lecturers and performing artists on foreign tours, increased attention to science and technology, and the development of a substantial exchange with the Soviet Union.

Despite its far fewer institutions for higher education, Britain had about the same number of foreign students and trainees in 1962 as the United States (60,000), three-quarters of them from less-developed nations. (Not all were university students; many were attending technical training institutes or learning on the job.) Whereas foreign students accounted for less than 2 per cent of total higher educational enrollments in the United States, in Great Britain they represented 8 per cent of university enrollments, 9 per cent in technical colleges and 3 per cent in teacher-training institutions.

Though only a small fraction of foreign students receive direct scholarship aid from the British government, virtually all are indirectly subsidized. The "hidden" costs of their education defrayed by tax funds flowing into British higher education have been estimated by the Overseas Development Institute at nearly £10 million annually. A large proportion benefit also from the advisory and hospitality services of the Council, which maintains twenty offices within the United Kingdom primarily to serve foreign students. The Council also administers a recent £3 million government grant to expand foreign student hostel and housing accommodations. No comparable services for foreign students are supported by the U.S. government.

The Council is the government's main instrument for handling other foreign guests and for sending distinguished lecturers, artists, writers, scientists, and other leading British figures on overseas tours. In the performing arts, the Council in 1961–62 financed twenty-three tours to thirty-five countries by some of the nation's finest musical and dramatic organizations.

The British support their overseas schools more generously than the United States, but less generously than the French and Germans (partly, perhaps, because over the years the British have placed more emphasis on training indigenous teachers for British-type schools). The Council now provides assistance to some 60 British-sponsored schools in 27 countries, mostly outside the Commonwealth.

British financial aid to educational development in the new nations (largely through agencies other than the Council) has concentrated—in contrast to French and American practice—on capital grants for new higher education facilities, mainly in the former British colonies of Africa. Since the war more than $30 million has been allocated for new higher technical colleges and university colleges, designed to become full-fledged universities eventually, as part of a calculated effort to prepare the colonies for independence.

That overseas demand for British teachers far exceeds the supply is due partly to the recruitment handicap imposed by the decentralized pattern of British education. "In this context," a recent British Council Report observed, "one cannot help but envy the French system under which teaching overseas is so much less of a career hazard than it has seemed in the past to teachers in Britain." The Council, with the aid of other official and professional organizations, is now making a major effort to expand the flow of teachers overseas. Faced with similar problems, the United States may find useful clues in this British experience.

Over-all, except for receiving foreign students and trainees, British educational aid to developing countries has been surprisingly small, both in absolute terms and as a percentage of total aid, considering the importance which the British generally attach to education. The Overseas Development Institute estimated that in 1962, through both bilateral and multilateral programs, the United Kingdom put only 6 per cent of its total aid effort (or about $30 million) into education and training projects. France has given education a decidedly higher priority in its aid program and, as nearly as one can judge from the inadequate facts available, so has the United States. In fairness it should be noted, however, that when British colonies achieved independence, most were better endowed with educational institutions (many built earlier with *private* British funds) and with well-educated local people, including teachers and administrators, than were most other European colonies.

Germany: New Aims and Old Methods

Germany's cultural relations policies have undergone a succession of striking changes over the past eighty years, reflecting major shifts in Germany's domestic politics and in its international posture and objectives. Some knowledge of this earlier experience is important to understanding the present situation.

In the first phase, from the 1880s to World War I, German cultural relations policy was focused almost entirely on Germans abroad and what came to be known as Germanism (*Deutschtum*). It was more concerned with nationalism and the quest for international influence and power than with cultural contacts with other peoples. The second phase began after World War I, in the bitter wake of the Treaty of Versailles. For the first time, with a small cultural section established in the Foreign Office, the German government adopted the policy of using German education and culture to influence not only overseas Germans but non-

Germans as well. It was essentially an effort to substitute cultural strength for the economic and military strength lost by the war. But the Weimar Republic did not have much time, and with Hitler came a new phase. He turned all the mechanisms of Germanism and of cultural relations—the overseas schools, churches and clubs, foreign student programs—to the service of Nazi propaganda, penetration, and subversion. That story is too familiar to need retelling.

In the fourth phase, under the postwar German Federal Republic, cultural relations at first languished, but within a few years the Bonn government was rapidly building a program. Between 1952 and 1960 the cultural budget of the foreign ministry rocketed from 2.8 million DM to 95.8 million DM (about $24 million). The prime aims were to build confidence among the nations of the West in the new government's peaceful intentions and democratic character; to show the world at large that Germany had been the land not merely of a Hitler but of Bach and Beethoven, of Kant and Goethe; and to restore the good will of those overseas Germans who were rudely disillusioned and disaffected by the Hitler era. In short, the aim was to recover Germany's lost world position and prestige, to begin the hard task of rebuilding good relations and good markets.

The recent phase, beginning about 1960, has been marked by an impressive further rise in the budget to 163 million DM in 1962, but more importantly by a broadened international outlook as shown, for example, by a heightened interest in aiding developing countries and by a more serious participation in UNESCO, involving many of Germany's leading cultural and scholarly groups. This new aim of moderating narrow nationalism among all nations—something quite new for Germany—was added to the old and continuing objectives of keeping strong ties with overseas Germans, building friends among foreigners, and enhancing Germany's prestige and economic position. In mood the new endeavors are in striking contrast to the frustration and bitterness which followed World War I and to the aggressive arrogance of the Hitler era. Yet Germany seems still to be in the process of clarifying its aims and adjusting actions to match them.

The actual pattern of the Federal Republic's cultural relations program does not seem to have caught up yet with the new objectives. For one thing, it is still narrow, both geographically and in the pattern of activities. German-sponsored schools abroad, for example, receive nearly one-third of the total cultural budget, and the bulk goes to a few countries (such as Brazil, Argentina, and Chile) where past German immigration was heaviest. It is a striking fact that in 1962 the Federal Republic gave fifteen times as much support to German-sponsored schools in Latin America as the U.S. government gave to American-sponsored schools there (about $3.8 million versus $250,000). The U.S. contribution was clearly inadequate, but one wonders if some of the German aid might not have been applied more usefully to the development of indigenous Latin American schools, to which the United States contributed vastly more.

The German cultural program puts strong emphasis on educational exchange. The Goethe Institute, which is private but supported by government, supplies German teachers and professors for service abroad, trains foreign teachers of German, and carries cultural programs overseas. University exchanges, financed by the Foreign Office, are handled by an inter-university exchange organization which has a high degree of autonomy. The interest of the German government in student exchanges is demonstrated by its recent commitment to bear half the future costs of the Fulbright exchange program. Germany is attracting more foreign students than ever before, despite serious problems for overcrowded German universities. The 24,000 foreign students studying in Germany in 1962—financed largely by nongovernment resources—constituted 10 per cent of total higher educational enrollments.

The German program of technical and educational assistance to developing countries, operated largely by several separate agencies outside the Foreign Office, has been considerably smaller than the French, British, and U.S. programs, but is now showing signs of expansion. Private efforts have considerably supplemented the modest government program. The language obstacle and the very limited colonial heritage of Germany have undoubtedly been important factors in holding down overseas educational and technical assistance aid, but it seems evident that

Germany has a considerably greater potential for rendering such aid than has thus far been exercised. Lately there have been mounting pressures from both within and without to use this potential more fully.

The Soviet Union: The Great Risk

Soviet cultural relations are in a class by themselves because they express Russia's unique political system, traditions, nationalism, and international aims. No nation, not even France, has made cultural affairs a more vital and integral part of its foreign policy or invested more generously in them. In so doing, the Soviet Union is perhaps taking a great political risk. In the decade since Stalin's death the Soviet cultural program has grown rapidly in scale, sophistication, and liberality. These recent trends, if continued, are likely to produce important changes not only in the U.S.S.R.'s external relations but within the Soviet society itself.

Historically, Soviet cultural relations have had sharp ups and downs. During the initial period of civil war—which coincided with Lenin's rule—the Soviet Union was culturally isolated from the outside world; but in 1925, with the revolution fairly well consolidated, a concerted effort was launched to tell the "new society's" story abroad, to win foreign friends, and to advance communism's international aims. The All-Union Society for Cultural Relations with Foreign Countries (known as VOKS) was established to promote Soviet "friendship societies" abroad and interchanges of various professional, artistic, and labor groups. Since the fledgling Soviet government enjoyed only limited diplomatic relations at the time and was generally considered a pariah by the older powers, cultural channels provided a means of bypassing governments and appealing directly to their peoples. One aim was to foster popular restraints upon such governments against hostile policies and acts toward the Soviet Union. Another was to strengthen the "progressive elements," and most of all the Communist organizations, within these other nations. By 1930 VOKS had developed cultural relations with private groups in seventy-seven nations, only forty-six of which had formal diplomatic relations with the Soviet Union.

These early efforts—a blend of genuine cultural interchange, politics, and propaganda—were often crudely ideological and, by Western standards, mutually contradictory. While advocating "cultural cooperation" on the one hand, Soviet officials also espoused the Marxist-Leninist view that "socialist culture" and "imperialist culture" were irreconcilably in conflict. The worldwide socialist revolution, they argued, must include a cultural revolution which would establish a "truly unified and universal human culture."

In the official Soviet view, then as now, scholarship, science, and the arts were inseparable from politics. Artists and scientists were expected to play their part in the movements for peace and for the popular front, and in other campaigns intended to promote the political aims of the U.S.S.R. Cultural societies abroad, as the Vice President of VOKS told a group of visiting Czech students in 1931, were to organize their work so as to attract such representatives of the working intelligentsia who, in times of great trial, could stand in defense of the U.S.S.R. "These societies must create a ring of trust, sympathy and friendship around the U.S.S.R., through which all plans of intervention will be unable to penetrate."[3]

The rise of fascism in the 1930s and the political purges within the Soviet Union itself led to a contraction of external cultural contacts, and the outbreak of World War II forced a still greater shrinkage. Late in the war, however, and immediately after, a fresh cultural effort was launched in support of the Soviet Union's postwar aims. It focused especially upon Latin America (where, for example, an ambitious new Russo-Mexican Cultural Institute was established in 1944 to promote Soviet cultural activities in the whole region) and upon neighboring small countries of Europe and the Near East where the Soviet Union's policies—viewed from the West as expansionist—were soon to precipitate a cold war with its wartime allies. Cultural activities of many sorts were stepped up. Over 500 scholarships for study in the Soviet Union were given in 1946 to students from Albania, Yugoslavia, Hungary, and other Eastern European countries;

[3] McMurry and Lee, cited, p. 117.

Soviet book exports reached impressive levels; Soviet friendship societies, pan-Slavic organizations and a constellation of anti-fascist committees were created or rejuvenated; and the flow of distinguished foreign visitors to Russia rose sharply. Cultural interchange remained, as earlier, the handmaiden of Soviet political aims. "Hitlerism has been smashed," a high Soviet official told a group of visiting Western scientists right after the war, "but the struggle against the remnants of reaction is continuing and no scientist who holds progress dear can remain aloof from this struggle."

The expanded cultural dialogue between East and West which immediately followed the defeat of Germany and gave great encouragement to many on both sides, proved, however, to be short-lived. With the hardening of the Stalinist line and the intensified cold war after 1948, the Soviet cultural curtain was once more drawn tight. Following Stalin's death in 1953 and the adoption of Khrushchev's "peaceful coexistence" line, however, the curtain began to lift again, this time higher than ever before. And despite recurrent political-military crises which seemed to belie the proclaimed policy of "peaceful coexistence," Soviet cultural interchanges with the West continued to expand. In the decade from 1953 to 1963 the Soviet government made a special effort to accumulate cultural treaties with the developing nations of Asia, Africa, and Latin America. For the first time, moreover, formal cultural exchange agreements were established with such Western powers as the United Kingdom and the United States.

With Soviet cultural relations thus becoming "normalized" through inter-governmental agreements, the old VOKS machinery was scrapped and a new State Committee for Cultural Relations with Foreign Countries was created as the central clearing house to coordinate all external exchange activities. Reflecting the importance attached by the Kremlin to these matters, this new State Committee is tied directly to the Council of Ministers; its head enjoys ministerial status and is empowered to secure the full cooperation of all ministries, academies, institutes, and non-governmental organizations concerned with educational, scientific, and cultural affairs. (It is as if, in the United States, the Bureau of Educational and Cultural Affairs were lifted out of the State Department, attached directly to the President's cabinet, endowed with full departmental status and given a clear mandate to establish policies and coordinate all international exchange activities, both governmental and private.)

Under these arrangements the Soviet cultural relations program has expanded rapidly and can be expected to continue growing as long as Khrushchev's policy of "peaceful coexistence" endures. The scale and diversity of this effort are suggested by the following examples:

In the fall of 1963, according to a high Soviet educational official, some 25,000 foreign students were enrolled in Soviet higher education, many from neighboring Communist nations but a sharply growing proportion from Africa, Asia, and Latin America. The typical foreign student is given full scholarship for four or five years. Many spend an initial year at the Patrice Lumumba Friendship University, learning Russian, remedying academic deficiencies, and otherwise being prepared for admission to the regular Soviet academic institutions.

Tourism to the Soviet Union has also grown by leaps and bounds in the past five years, and most Western visitors have apparently encountered fewer restraints on their freedom of movement than anticipated, despite some dramatic exceptions, which did incalculable harm to the Soviet cultural relations effort.

Even more significant, perhaps, has been the new phenomenon of Soviet citizens going abroad as tourists. Some 10,000, for example, were permitted to attend the Brussels Fair in 1958. It seems likely that the United States will receive a good number of nonofficial Soviet tourists in the next few years, provided the present severe stringency of Soviet foreign currency supply is relieved.

The Soviet overseas book program has also expanded rapidly. According to official figures, exports rose from about 27 million books (698 separate titles) in 1958 to over 40 million (1,068 titles in 34 foreign languages) in 1961. A much larger number of books was produced abroad with Soviet financial assistance, for sale usually at below-cost prices. All told, USIA analysts believe it to be "a reasonable assumption that some 150 million books in free-world languages were produced by the Soviet Union (directly and indirectly) for distribution abroad in 1961." Not all of these books are of Communist origin, though they are obviously selected with an eye to advancing the Soviet cause.

The Soviet Union has been pre-eminent in sending its best artistic talent abroad for cultural presentations. (I suspect that the Bolshoi and Moiseyev ballet companies and the Leningrad Symphony Orchestra, for example, have lately built more good will for the Soviet Union in Europe, the United States, and Latin America than all the VOKS bulletins and other earlier propaganda activities combined.) In the less developed countries, especially in Asia, the Soviet Union has cultivated the good will of local audiences (and spread political ideas) with its traveling circuses, trained bear acts, puppet shows, and other folksy entertainment groups.

The Soviet cultural relations effort also emphasizes appreciation for the artistic and literary accomplishments of other nations. The enthusiastic and sometimes almost unrestrained reception by Soviet audiences, of American singers, musicians, and art exhibits have been matched by the flattering attention paid them by high Soviet officials. Chairman Khrushchev's occasionally picturesque criticisms of American modern art and jazz have served mainly to emphasize that he took the trouble to attend a U.S. concert or exhibit. The Soviet Union also makes much of the artists and writers of developing countries. Many performing groups of folk dancers, singers, and the like are invited to the Soviet Union and are well received. Many Latin American writers, who have felt ignored and unappreciated by the United States, are naturally pleased and impressed to have their works translated in the Soviet Union and elsewhere in Eastern Europe—and to receive generous royalty payments.

The Soviet cultural relations effort places great emphasis at home on the learning of foreign languages by the Soviet people, not merely by specialists but by "the masses" as well. The younger Soviet experts one encounters around the world today have significantly better foreign language skills than their elders and are accordingly more effective in their work and personal relationships (though this applies mainly to those trained for diplomacy rather than for technical specialties). The Soviet Union is now developing a few hundred special schools in which Soviet children will receive virtually their entire education, from the first grade on, in a foreign language. Such schools already exist for the more widely used languages, such as English, French, Chinese, Spanish, Arabic, and Hindi; but others will soon embrace less familiar languages of Asia and Africa, some of which are known in the United States only by a mere handful of specialized scholars and are taught, if at all, only in the graduate schools of universities. One can well imagine the advantages that this investment in foreign language schools will have some years hence for Soviet cultural, commercial, and political relations all over the world.

Since Stalin's death the Soviet Union has joined UNESCO and is taking the work of this organization seriously. It has provided a number of first-rate experts to serve in the UNESCO secretariat and on UNESCO missions. The Soviet Union has also expanded considerably its educational aid and technical assistance to developing countries. Recently, for example, it has built and staffed an advanced technical training institute in India and is operating important educational projects in Afghanistan and Mali. Many foreign trainees are brought to the Soviet Union for specialized training, usually in how to operate or maintain Soviet-type industrial facilities or products in their home countries.

This impressive array of cultural, scientific, and educational activities, similar in form to many American activities, is aimed at several Soviet objectives, only some of them associated with the cold war. The most fundamental aim, of course, is to strengthen Soviet world power and prestige, to advance Soviet aims and influence in selected countries, and to augment Communist strength wherever possible. It is noteworthy that the Soviet cultural effort, in contrast to that of the United States, tends to concentrate on selected countries, presumably those of greatest importance to Soviet foreign policy objectives. Mexico, Cuba, and Venezuela, for example, have long received more attention than most other Latin American countries, and several former French colonies in Africa today receive more attention than most former British colonies. Within these selected countries, again in some contrast to American practice, there is a heavy concentration of attention upon selected key groups and individuals, such as youth leaders, labor leaders, writers and other intellectuals. Although the Soviet Union has an impressive foreign broadcasting program and is expanding its film program (especially in Africa), less of its total effort is spent on trying to influence mass opinion directly. Relatively more is directed at strategic local people who are shapers of popular attitudes and political developments.

It is noteworthy also that today the Soviet cultural program, at least with respect to exchanges with advanced Western countries, is less obviously preoccupied with propaganda and immediate political matters than during the prewar period. There is heavier emphasis now on genuine intellectual, technical, and artistic exchange without immediate ideological connotations, though certainly considerations of ideology and national interest are always present. There may be several reasons for this change. One is that the Soviet Union, still much concerned with its own economic development, is anxious to acquire useful scientific and technical knowledge from other countries; another is that it clearly suits the current policy of "peaceful coexistence." Present Soviet leadership appears to have concluded that communizing the Western nations is not a practical goal for the foreseeable future and is therefore pursuing a strategy of accommodation. How long this policy will last is still an open question, but the improved mutual understanding that is gradually being brought about by these interchanges is certainly helping to create conditions that will make any other policy increasingly difficult.

From all appearances, Soviet leaders are finding it more important to justify their policies and actions to their own people; and the better educated and informed the people become, the greater this necessity is likely to be. Indeed, it appears that one other objective of the present Soviet cultural program is to demonstrate to the Soviet people themselves that their government is on good terms with others and is pursuing a peaceful course.

The Soviet cultural effort is not without its difficulties, some being similar to those encountered by the United States and other Western nations. Soviet technical assistance officials, for example, have by now discovered that rendering aid is often a very difficult, frustrating, and thankless business, regardless of one's ideology. But the Soviet Union also has its unique problems. With respect to foreign students, for example, it not only has a serious language barrier to overcome but frequently is obliged to accept less well qualified students who have been unsuccessful in securing an opportunity to study in Western Europe or the United States. And ironically, the Soviet Union, which officially denies the existence of race prejudice, seems to be having much greater difficulty on this score with African students than the United States, which freely admits to having a race relations problem and is trying to do something about it.

Another special problem of the Soviet Union is posed by the bureaucratic complexities, rigidities, and delays which inevitably result from trying to handle all external cultural relations through government channels. Some of the difficulties encountered in the U.S.-U.S.S.R. exchange program which are popularly attributed to political motives are, I am convinced, more bureaucratic than political in origin.

The most fundamental problem for the Soviet Union, however, is how fast and how far to move toward relaxing restrictions upon a full and free interchange of people, ideas, and knowledge with other nations. By previous standards there has been a marked liberalization in recent years. Yet Soviet officials are still far from ready to permit the kind of uninhibited flow of books, films, magazines, broadcasts, and people that has long been taken for granted among the nations of Western Europe and North America, and among many developing nations as well. It is exceedingly difficult, as Adlai Stevenson has pointed out, to keep a closed society closed. Even more difficult is to open it part way, as has now been done, and to continue to control the situation thereafter. Beyond a certain point the process of opening up becomes irreversible and then uncontrollable. Thus, despite the evident short-run values which increased cultural exchanges have for the Soviet Union, the long-run inevitably involves a risk. By its very nature cultural interchange is the natural enemy of ideological rigidities and of closed societies. Soviet leaders must surely realize this. Their very willingness to take the gamble is itself cause for encouragement.

A particularly fascinating question right now, of course, is whether the serious deterioration of Soviet-Chinese relations will accelerate or retard the liberalization of Soviet cultural relations with the West. Thus far, this struggle within the Communist family appears to be favoring rather than discouraging a greater cultural rapprochement with the so-called capitalist nations.

Conclusions

It is difficult and risky to attempt a detailed comparison of different national efforts in international educational and cultural affairs, but a few general conclusions seem warranted. As to absolute size, the over-all American effort, including private activities, is undoubtedly larger than that of any other nation; but relative to national resources and foreign commitments and obligations, our public activity in this field is smaller than that of the Soviet Union or France and perhaps smaller even than that of Germany and the United Kingdom.

The European nations, especially the Soviet Union and France, obviously take cultural affairs more seriously as a dimension of their foreign policy than does the United States. They do so, quite evidently, not out of woolly-headed sentiment or starry-eyed idealism, but because they are convinced that a large investment in cultural relations pays off in very practical terms. It is ironic that those Americans who fancy themselves hard-headed realists have been slow to reach this same conclusion. The practical men of Congress who more than a century ago created the land-grant college system as a means to develop America's internal strengths would probably be the first to recognize the importance today of using educational means to develop America's external strengths.

One other contrast is worth noting, namely, that in this field the Americans and British are relatively less nationalistic and more international and universal in their approach than the French, Germans, and Russians, and in this respect are perhaps more realistic than the others, in view of the broad thrust of world history. Given the vast changes in the world since the last war, the narrowly nationalistic strategy of cultural relations that was followed in the nation-state system of the nineteenth century is no longer appropriate, especially for great powers whose interests lie in building a strong and harmonious international community.

Chapter V

What Has Been Achieved?

The nations discussed in the preceding chapter have evidently found that cultural relations are a worthwhile endeavor. Can the same be said for the United States? Have the American educational and cultural activities described in earlier chapters been worth the money and the effort? Have they advanced the objectives of U.S. foreign policy?

My own broad-brush appraisal is that they have been a fruitful and practical investment. Indeed, I would go so far as to say that, dollar for dollar, they have often yielded more than our far larger national outlays for foreign economic and military aid. But the record also has its imperfections. The educational and cultural efforts have sometimes been poorly aimed and missed their mark. The experience with France, discussed below, may be a case in point. There have also been instances of serious under-investment, along with a failure of nerve and imagination, of which Latin America may be an example. And almost every-where the results could have been improved had the total program been better planned and more coherently conducted.

Despite these shortcomings, however, the over-all picture is one of impressive accomplishment. There are many encouraging examples of developments to which our cultural policies have made a vital contribution: the reorientation of Germany and Japan since the war, the continuing advance of India along democratic lines, and the building of long-term mutual understanding with such new nations as Burma and Indonesia despite fickle political winds. Further examples are the initial good will established with the new African nations, the strengthening of ties among Western nations, and the beginnings of a productive dialogue with the Soviet Union and other Communist nations. The acid test for many is whether the educational component of U.S. foreign policy has helped significantly toward ending the cold war on acceptable terms and improving the prospects for a stable peace. Here again the evidence is, on balance, distinctly favorable.

Such assessments, of course, cannot be made with mathematical accuracy; they must be matters of judgment. And judgments necessarily require interpretations of history and current trends on which there can be honest differences of opinion. But if we are to extract lessons from the past, we must be willing to venture upon interpretations. Anyone who examines objectively the abundance of available evidence, country by country, and who has the opportunity to make extensive personal observations, is likely to reach the general conclusion stated above, though his judgment may differ on individual cases. To reinforce this conclusion let us turn first to the best body of evidence yet assembled and then examine a few specific cases.

A comprehensive and authoritative evaluation of the subject was made for Congress in 1963 by the U.S. Advisory Commission on International Educational and Cultural Affairs, known as the Gardner Commission.[1] Although this study was limited to the exchange-of-persons program of the Department of State, its findings have important implications for the entire educational component of U.S. foreign policy. The conclusions, summarized below in the Commission's own words, are based upon interviews and other direct evidence from several thousand persons who had participated in exchanges in a cross-section of twenty countries, plus testimony from dozens of U.S. ambassadors and foreign service officers and numerous American educational leaders.

Testimony is overwhelming from all sources that the program as a whole is effective. The Commission was frankly surprised, though

[1] *A Beacon of Hope—The Exchange-of-Persons Program,* A Report from the U.S. Advisory Commission on International Educational and Cultural Affairs (Washington: GPO, 1963). Anyone seriously interested in having a competent and comprehensive assessment of the exchange of persons will find the Advisory Commission's report required reading. Not only is it well written and cogently presented, but its conclusions are fortified throughout with concrete and persuasive evidence.

gratified, at the wealth, variety and convincing character of the evidence. . . .

The evidence is also conclusive that the program has proved itself an essential and valuable part of America's total international effort. The basic concept of the program, its potential in accomplishing a wide variety of essential and desirable ends, were overwhelmingly endorsed.

In looking for results that contributed directly to major U.S. foreign policy objectives, the Commission found "impressive," "abundant" and "conclusive" evidence that the exchange program:

. . . increases mutual understanding . . . has succeeded in helping dispel among foreign visitors many misconceptions and ugly stereotypes about the American people.

. . . has been outstandingly successful in providing a valuable educational experience to foreign grantees.

. . . has also benefited [the grantee's] home country.

. . . has effectively established channels of communication between the people in other countries and the United States.

. . . has effectively supported one of the nation's most basic international objectives—of helping support strong free societies able to work together, in mutual trust and understanding, on the grave issues of our time.

Though its over-all appraisal was highly favorable, the Gardner Commission found significant weaknesses in the exchange program and made numerous recommendations for improvement. These will be considered in the final chapter.

Let us extend the appraisal now to an assortment of coutries and areas, each of which presents unique circumstances for U.S. foreign policy. I have chosen mainly those with which I have had some first-hand experience, but in all cases I have leaned heavily upon the judgments of others better qualified than I am to support my interpretations and conclusions.

Germany and Japan—The Reorientation of Totalitarian Systems

Nowhere has the educational and cultural approach played such a prominent role in U.S. foreign policy, or more nearly reached a "saturation effort," than in the postwar attempt to re-orient Germany and Japan from their aggressive and totalitarian past to a peaceful and democratic future. This was an exceed-ingly difficult, complex and subtle task for which the United States was poorly prepared by experience, and for which conven-tional political, economic and military instruments of foreign policy were clearly inadequate. Under the circumstances, re-sponsible American officials—such men as John J. McCloy, Gen-eral MacArthur, General Lucius Clay, and James B. Conant—turned instinctively to America's own deep faith and experience in education.

It is easy now to forget how massive and unique this effort was—much greater than any before or since. Hundreds of Ger-man and Japanese leaders and potential leaders in many walks of life were invited to the United States to get acquainted with American democratic values, institutions, and processes. In turn, many American experts stationed in the occupied nations de-voted untold energies to the task of helping to reshape their edu-cational, political, cultural and economic institutions along democratic lines. Much of this work was done at the local level, thanks to the fact of occupation, and therefore more likely to be lasting than mere declarations and speeches at the top. It was important, however, that officials of the highest rank put their full weight behind the effort in a manner never equaled since. General Eisenhower and High Commissioner McCloy, for ex-ample, made special trips to Washington to persuade congres-sional appropriations committees of the need for larger funds for educational and cultural measures, and Congress responded gen-erously.

By and large, these efforts were amply justified by the results. Indeed, in the whole history of officially sponsored U.S. educa-tional and cultural relations, Germany and Japan probably rep-resent the clearest success stories. There were, of course, mistakes and at times embarrassing amateurishness (as, for example, when American educators sought to impose local school boards and other ill-fitting U.S. models on Japan). Some of the changes and reforms did not long survive the occupation, as traditional Ger-man or Japanese patterns were bound to reassert themselves. But anyone who visits Germany or Japan today with a perceptive eye and ready ear cannot help but be impressed by the observable results. This is not to say that all vestiges of the totalitarian past have yet been wiped out. Nor is it to claim that our policies in Germany and Japan succeeded mainly because of our re-education efforts; the credit due them on that score remains a matter of considerable debate. Yet there is little doubt that the American educational and cultural activities did make a fundamental contribution to establishing a democratic way of life and achieving results which could not have been attained by other means.

The continuation of interchanges after the occupation period, increasingly through private channels, has also had substantial results. U.S. Ambassador Reischauer, the eminent scholar-diplomat who had known Japan intimately for many years, told the Gardner Commission in 1963, "I believe that the wide intellectual contacts developed between Japanese and Americans since the end of the American occupation a decade ago are one of the major reasons why we are at present witnessing a gradual shift of Japanese attitudes and opinions away from doctrinaire Marxism toward a position that we would regard as more desirable."

There is obviously a variety of reasons why the Federal Republic of Germany has consistently and strongly supported American foreign policy in recent years, but it is not without significance that nearly one-third of the 520 members elected to the German Bundestag in 1961 and over half the upper chamber (as well as ten members of Chancellor Adenauer's 1962 Cabinet) had been participants in the U.S. "leader exchange" program. The U.S. Ambassador to Germany in 1962 characterized the exchange program as "one of the most effective tools for developing understanding and support of the United States and free world institutions and objectives."

At the U.S.-Japanese Educational and Cultural Conference in 1962, arranged by President Kennedy and Prime Minister Ikeda, outstanding intellectual leaders of both nations reviewed systematically the progress made since the war in American-Japanese relations through educational and cultural channels. All agreed that the gains had been large, with important benefits to both nations. Just before going to this conference I was asked sternly by some members of a Senate Committee why U.S. taxpayers' money should be spent to bring Japanese labor leaders to the United States. Wouldn't U.S. labor unions, they asked, simply teach the Japanese unions bad habits, such as striking? And were we not simply supplying these Japanese "radicals" (which, indeed, some were) with more ammunition to criticize us? At lunch in Tokyo just after that I asked a conservative Japanese banker whether he thought these labor exchanges were useful and should be continued. Again at dinner that evening I asked the same question of a reputedly radical Japanese labor leader. Both answered quickly in the affirmative and seemed surprised that I should even ask, in view of the clearly demonstrated benefits, as they saw it, to both countries.

The banker said that the example of American labor unions exerted a moderating influence on the extreme left wing of Japanese organized labor, encouraged more democracy in union affairs, and shifted organized labor's attention from politics to collective bargaining and the improvement of the workers' economic welfare. This tended, he admitted, to raise wages and costs and perhaps to weaken somewhat Japan's competitive position in world markets, but it was a small price to pay for politically responsible unionism. The labor leader, who had been a vigorous critic of the United States, said his visit to this country had considerably modified his views, and on his return he had helped change the views of others. Among the things that impressed him most were: "the wonderful atmosphere of your public schools . . . the astonishing respect Americans have for their flag . . . the reasons why Americans don't like communism . . . and the preoccupation of your labor unions with improving working conditions, without becoming company unions." Then he added, "I am still critical of some U.S. policies and practices, but now more likely for the right reasons, I think." And he had become much more critical of Communist China's policies. "You would be well advised," he concluded, "to continue these labor exchanges."

The distractions and frustrations of the cold war have tended to make us forget the vital role played by all types of exchanges in bringing Japan and Germany quite successfully through the occupation period and into the democratic family. The danger now is that we will take these nations for granted and relax our efforts at mutual understanding, just because their present governments generally support our foreign policies. But there are restless forces in both nations that America needs to understand better, for they are almost certain to have great future influence upon the policies of these countries. It could prove the height of folly, for example, to close U.S. libraries in Germany, to shrink the labor union exchanges with Japan, and otherwise to lessen our educational and cultural exchanges with them. Yet this is exactly what we have lately been doing. No one realizes the danger better than responsible German and Japanese officials. They have expressed concern over these reductions and, in Germany's case, offered to share future costs of the necessary means for maintaining mutual understanding.

Latin America—For Want of a Neighborly Dialogue

If we need a reminder of the folly of taking friends for granted, we can find it in Latin America. It was here that the U.S. cultural relations program got its start, yet it is here also, ironically, that our postwar efforts have fallen most conspicuously short of the need and opportunity. To be sure, many useful things have been done; one can find dozens of good examples. But in the aggregate the program throughout the 1950s was grossly inadequate and unimaginative.

A visitor to Latin America discovers alongside abundant good will ugly misconceptions and deep bitterness toward the United States, which are readily translated into hostile political forces. Basically these are the bitter fruits of the gross social and economic inequities that still prevail in much of Latin America. But in the eyes of the restless and discontented, the United States stands guilty of too long tolerating and abetting the powerful elites that have resisted the correction of these inequities, and of itself exploiting an unequal relationship.

The intellectuals of Latin America—loosely defined to include writers, scholars, educators, journalists, artists, labor leaders, and youth leaders—are the main rebels against the *status quo,* the severest critics of the United States, and in the long run the most powerful agents of social and political change. Castro was one of these, as were many of his present collaborators, long before most of them turned to communism. The tragedy is that so many of these intellectuals were for so long seriously out of communication with their counterparts in the United States, who, except for a relative handful, were too preoccupied with other matters and other areas to pay much attention to Latin America. Here was a case where the U.S. government might well have called upon the private sector for more help, in addition to expanding the State Department's exchange program and handling it with more boldness and imagination.

But until recently our official appraisals and prescriptions attached too little importance to achieving a deeper understanding of the United States by its intellectual critics in Latin America, thereby demonstrating that on our side there was need also for understanding these critics better. Indeed, in the era of McCarthyism the tendency of U.S. embassies in Latin America was to ban the left-leaning intellectuals from the exchange program and otherwise steer clear of them. As it turned out, some of these "radicals" were advocating nothing more than the very aims and principles that finally came to be embodied in the Alliance for Progress in 1961. Others, propelled by well-cultivated misconceptions and innocent of any first-hand knowledge of the United States because our government had kept them out, moved further to the left and today are the leading *Fidelistas* in many countries of Latin America. It seems no wild speculation to say that had the Alliance been launched ten or even five years earlier, and had it included an imaginative emphasis on educational development and on intellectual and cultural interchange, the social and political situation today in Latin America might be considerably less fraught with danger.

Now the need is better recognized and somewhat more is being done, yet even the current endeavors seem grossly and dangerously inadequate. Those who insist on holding the line on the State Department's exchange budget are assuming responsibility for grave risks which may well lead to far heavier costs in the future. The several U.S. ambassadors to Latin America whose opinions I know on this subject are all agreed that there is need for a more concerted educational and cultural effort aimed at developing educational opportunities in Latin America, at broadening the dialogue between our intellectuals and theirs, and at deepening the understanding between North and South America. A number of well-informed Senators and Representatives concur very strongly in this view, while others still refuse to face the facts.

One of the most knowledgeable of the respondents to the U.S. Advisory Commission summed it up very well:

> Economic and social reform . . . in Latin America and the Caribbean to which the Alliance for Progress is addressed—will be feasible only to the extent that attitudes are changed in the realm of politics and policies, that intelligence is challenged and upgraded, and that the development of human resources is accomplished. These are immense undertakings in which foreign (and especially U.S.) intervention and assistance are a difficult and delicate enterprise politically. The somewhat indirect and oblique, but vitally essential, approach through education and cultural affairs is the most welcomed and accepted, the least likely to be resented, or suspected, the most potent long-range.[2]

Nowhere are the common sense of our foreign policy and the potentialities of our educational and intellectual resources more fully challenged today than in Latin America. There may yet be time to recover lost ground, but there surely is no time to waste.

India and Indonesia—The Saving Thread of Educational Exchange

Any American who has spent time in India during the past decade, talking with government officials, journalists, scholars, and young people, is likely to be somewhat more optimistic than the average American newspaper reader about the long-run prospects for U.S.-Indian relations and the ultimate success of India's great experiment in democracy. At least until Communist China's aggression in 1962, the headlines focused mainly upon the touchier issues of U.S.-Indian political relations, such as U.S. military aid to Pakistan, our China policy, our neutrality in the

2 *A Beacon of Hope—The Exchange-of-Persons Program,* cited, pp. 56–57.

Kashmir issue, and India's relative silence on such issues as Berlin, Hungary, and the resumption of Soviet nuclear tests. But beneath these surface tensions many things were occurring to draw the Indian and American peoples closer together and to strengthen India's resolution to maintain the democratic approach in meeting its unbelievably massive problems. The U.S. government's educational programs in India and the substantial efforts of private U.S. foundations and other organizations have played a major role in these salutary developments.

The great rapport between Indians and Americans, which began with private educational and missionary efforts long ago, has been steadily strengthened since India's independence by private and governmental activities involving hundreds of institutions and thousands of individuals in both countries. There is not an Indian university, I dare say, that in the past ten years has not had a dozen or more American scholars in residence, and virtually every American university, in turn, has had several times this number of Indian guests. Practically every Indian ministry at the state as well as federal level has had American technical experts working side by side with its own officials. Important new institutions have been created in India with U.S. help in such fields as public administration, economic development, English language teaching, vocational education, and village development. There has been a substantial two-way exchange of artistic performances, often through private channels.

Though usually thought of as "aid to India," the flow of benefits from all these activities has in fact been in both directions. Through first-hand experience in India a great many Americans—scholars, government officials, businessmen, and ordinary tourists—have had their eyes and minds opened, as well as their hearts, to the problems and aspirations of the underdeveloped two-thirds of the world. In the process, American competence to deal more effectively with world problems has been immeasurably enhanced.

Indonesia provides an example of how educational and cultural activities, in a peculiarly unstable and frustrating political context, can sometimes be the strongest and most viable instrument available to U.S. foreign policy. What goes on quietly beneath the ruffled political surface may in the long run be of greatest importance. Attorney General Robert Kennedy was quick to recognize this fact when he visited Indonesia in 1962 and returned to urge a strengthening of U.S. educational and cultural programs.

In visiting Indonesia myself a few years ago for the Ford Foundation, I was impressed by the evident affinity and sympathy that exist between Americans and Indonesians, even though their cultural backgrounds are literally half a world apart. Despite occasional disruptive efforts by a few Indonesian politicians—who thought they saw more in communism than in democracy (though in reality thay had had little opportunity to discover what either was really about)—American professors and educators continued to work with Indonesian educators and students, and with many government officials, in an atmosphere of mutual confidence and respect, even in such sensitive areas as the social sciences.

The American contribution to Indonesian education and the attendant influence of American ideas upon many Indonesian leaders have already been considerable. Nearly all of the present younger deputy ministers, for example, who constitute the top echelon of Indonesia's civil service, attended U.S. colleges and universities. Unlike India, Indonesia entered independence without a well-developed civil service or a reasonably well-functioning and vertically integrated educational system. These essential elements of viable nationhood are still in the making—all too slowly. Without adequately developed institutions and human resources the economy of Indonesia cannot reach the point of self-sustained growth, the government cannot function efficiently and effectively, and political maturity cannot be achieved. In the circumstances, there can be no better long-range investment for the United States than to help develop the knowledge and skills of Indonesia's people and the institutions on which their independence and progress can rest. Such investment now, without political strings but with patience and compassion, holds higher promise of benefiting both nations in the long run than any other available course of action.

Africa—A Leap Across Centuries

Though very different from Indonesia in many respcts, Ethiopia is another instance where educational and cultural activities are one of the most promising means available to U.S. foreign policy. After 3,000 years of independence, Ethiopia still stands, by any measure, as one of the least developed nations of Africa, groping its way toward modernization. Yet it is also a nation with ample resources and considerable potential, worthy of serious attention and help.

Only a tiny fraction of Ethiopia's population has had any formal education at all. Indeed, I was told by an important churchman that a high proportion of the Coptic priests is illiterate, and that in some church schools in remote villages children are still taught that the world is flat. But by now there are several hundred younger people, living mostly in Addis Ababa, who have acquired a college education—some in the local university college and many abroad, particularly in the United States. Almost without exception these younger people have a marked desire and impatience to accelerate the pace of modernization. Many of their influential elders, and most particularly the Emperor with whom I was privileged to discuss the matter, also desire modernization and regard education as a major means; but, being perhaps more sensitive to the disturbing changes in the social, economic and political power structure that modernization implies, they are inclined to move more slowly. Thus there is a marked schism between the older generation that still holds power and the younger group of educated civilians and military officers who want to move faster. This schism was dramatically demonstrated in the short-lived military coup of 1961.

The young "radicals" of Ethiopia are, by and large, not Marxists or revolutionaries but simply intelligent patriots seized by the Western concepts of progress and social justice. A few hundred of them turned up, in and out of uniform, at a unique reception given for "American alumni" at the U.S. Embassy in Addis Ababa while I was there in 1961. They talked eagerly about their "alma mater" in the United States, what they had learned and what they had been able, or unable, to do with this learning upon returning home. There was evident frustration, however, and a reluctance to speak openly about their own nation's needs and problems (though in private they were far more voluble). Later in an off-the-record seminar with student leaders at the university college I found the same friendly attitude, the same eagerness to discuss ideas freely with an outsider, and the same sense of frustration and keenness to get on with the job of modernizing Ethiopia.

I was struck by their lack of hostility toward those in power, especially the Emperor, yet their criticism and impatience with the slowness of change. They had no doctrinaire solutions, no ideological panaceas. They wanted action—precisely what sort they wanted was not clear—and they looked especially to the United States for encouragement and help. Meanwhile, not surprisingly, Soviet officials were that very weekend inaugurating a new film center in Addis Ababa to serve Ethiopia and neighboring African countries. The feature film showed Major Gagarin's recent space flight. And down the street the Soviet library was crowded with curious young Ethiopians.

It was plain to see that this substantial group of college-educated people in their twenties and thirties represented the "New Ethiopia" and that before many years they would be in power. What they will do then will obviously depend heavily upon the attitudes and insights they have formed through their education and their contacts with the outside world. They seemed, therefore, a much more crucial investment than the jet airport which the United States had just helped build on the edge of Addis Ababa, or the fighter planes it provided to the Ethiopian Air Force. It was encouraging soon afterward to see the Peace Corps enter Ethiopia on a substantial scale, more than doubling that country's meager supply of secondary school teachers almost overnight.

Despite America's highly publicized racial problems which regularly command banner headlines in Africa and Asia, and despite the tardy and feeble start of its cultural activities in sub-Saharan Africa, the United States has a strong attraction for Africans. American education is already having an important impact there, especially in the former British colonies where English is spoken.

Nigeria, a dynamic society, is a bellwether among the newly independent African nations. Its well-educated political leaders place a high priority on education, higher, for example, than do the leaders of most Latin American countries. They are aware both of its popular appeal and of its indispensability to economic, social and political development. Nigeria's British-type educational system is impressively good as far as it goes. But in important respects it is poorly suited to the development needs and the scarce resources of this new nation. What countries like Nigeria need, and many of their leaders realize it, is not simply a larger educational system but a different one, tailored to their circumstances.

Nigeria, like several other new African nations, has turned to the United States for help. Even more than money they want imaginative ideas and access to talent. While valuing highly the considerable good that came to them—and is still coming to them—from British education, they want to fashion a more relevant curriculum and more efficient and effective teaching methods (including very unconventional ones if necessary) which will serve far more students, better and sooner. They do not want to replace a British-type system with a carbon copy of the American; they want to design their own. They also want help on filling key teaching posts in secondary and higher education until they can build an adequate staff of their own, in part by sending their young people to the United States, England, and elsewhere for advanced education beyond Nigeria's present capacities.

There are already many American teachers, professors, and educational experts in Nigeria (including Peace Corps volunteers), and numerous Nigerians are studying in the United States who will shortly return home as builders and leaders of their nation. Especially encouraging and effective have been the strong initiatives taken by private U.S. foundations and the close working relations which are being established directly between Nigeria and American universities. Another encouraging factor has been the cooperative attitude of British officials and educators, who, far from resenting American participation, have urged more of it.

Kenya, being smaller and more recently independent, presents a somewhat different situation, but like Nigeria it attaches the highest value to education and looks to the United States as a major source of help. Because of the enthusiasm of Tom Mboya and other political leaders, Kenya, for its size, has sent more students to the United States in recent years than any other African country.

The influx of African students has created a rash of practical problems for the American hosts, but also a rash of opportunities. Most of all, it has imposed enormous responsibilities on the American colleges and communities involved, for the personal experiences these students have in the United States, both academically and socially, can greatly influence the course of U.S.-African relations in the future. The surprising fact thus far is not that difficulties have arisen but that things have gone as well as they have. The record of American educators working in Africa, and of African students studying in the United States, is on the whole a remarkably encouraging one.

The progress in so short a time and the prognosis are favorable, though obviously Nigeria and Kenya, and other African states as well, still face formidable problems. Though the American effort has grown considerably in the last three years, it is still grossly inadequate. How the United States responds in the next few years to further requests of African nations for educational help can make a decisive difference ten or twenty years from now in the economic and social gains these nations make, in their political stability and complexion, and in their future relations with the Western nations. If the response is judicious and generous, tomorrow's historians are likely to label education as America's most strategic investment in the new Africa of the 1960s. It will not guarantee that on international issues the African states will always stand with us; on the contrary, their neutralism is likely to endure for some time. There is no doubt, however, that as the educational and cultural ties now being created are strengthened and developed, the areas of common political and economic interest will grow along with them.

France—The Baffling Case

The postwar educational and cultural exchange experience between the United States and France proves that the character and quality of such programs are more important than the quantity. Since World War II hundreds of students and scholars have been exchanged between the two nations, but the available evidence leaves much doubt as to whether this interchange has actually been as effective as it might have been in strengthening their mutual understanding. Some good has certainly come of it, but compared to other countries the exchange program with France seems to have been less effective.

About the evidence there is little doubt. The U.S. Advisory Commission found, as did various earlier investigators, that the reaction of French participants in the exchange to their stay in the United States was distinctly less favorable and more critical than the attitudes of those from other nations, including Western European ones. A considerably higher proportion of the French took a dim view of American education, art and music, for example, and doubted that the experience had been rewarding professionally or personally. So striking is the French exception that the Gardner Commission observed, "The unique character of French reactions to many aspects of the State Department program, particularly the educational aspects, were indeed so great as to suggest the possible need for a wholly different approach for France."[3]

Why should this be so? I have asked a number of perceptive French friends for their explanation, and while their answers differed somewhat, three main points stood out. First, they noted, is the high esteem which every educated Frenchman is bred to have for his nation's rich and distinguished culture. For some this self-esteem becomes disdain for other cultures. A second contributing factor is the psychological hangover from the traumatic experience which the French, as a great and proud nation, underwent in World War II and more recently in the loss of their overseas territories. But the third factor suggested by these

3 Cited, p. 59.

French observers is perhaps the most significant. It is that French society itself has been undergoing a profound internal change since the war which has sharply divided two major intellectual groups, the "humanists" and the "scientists and technologists." Members of the former group, they note, are today defending the bastions of French cultural superiority. They are prompted to take a defensive and narrowly nationalistic posture and to make anti-Americanism a favorite sport. The scientific-technical group, on the other hand, has become the more creative force in French culture, has contributed greatly to the remarkable rise in French productivity and national income in recent years, and therefore has no feeling of defensiveness. On the contrary, like the great creative French artists and writers of an earlier day, they feel part of an international community, they have no hesitation to acknowledge the accomplishments of others or to cooperate with them, and they openly admire American accomplishments.

If this explanation is accurate, or largely so, then it may be that the U.S. educational exchange effort in the case of France has been misdirected. Perhaps it aimed so hard at the target—to persuade the French that the United States, too, had a culture worthy of respect—that it missed. Possibly the exchange program has concentrated to heavily on the very Frenchmen, the men of arts and letters, who cared little about American cultural attainments, and too lightly on those more concerned with finding a basis for mutual understanding, cooperation, and respect between the two nations. Perhaps the scales were similarly tipped in the selection of American scholars going to France. Had more attention been given to exchanging the more creative talent rather than the merely critical and the discontented, the results might perhaps have been more gratifying.

This explanation would, of course, be considered rank heresy by many humanistic scholars in both lands. But whatever the correct explanation may be, this unique situation bears further looking into, and in the process we might learn things worth knowing about both contemporary French society and our own.

We have to realize, too, that between two major Western countries like France and the United States an official cultural exchange program can play but a small part in the totality of their relationship. In the cultural field alone—leaving aside the more weighty considerations involving security, alliances, trade, and finance—officially sponsored exchanges are a minor element in a stream of contacts of many kinds, most of which have nothing to do with the two governments. It is this broad stream which provides most of the cultural content in the relations of the two countries. A government may attempt to guide, exploit, or draw on it, but cannot easily control it in the interests of its foreign policy.

What About the Cold War?

Many Americans have one simple test of the value of any international activity—does it help us win the cold war? More than once I was asked in congressional appropriations hearings: "How many countries have your exchange programs kept from slipping behind the Iron Curtain? . . . Give us concrete evidence to prove, even in one single case, that these programs have helped defeat communism. . . . Explain to us just how a professor going to Africa or a fiddle player going to Latin America can help us fight communism? . . . Wouldn't the money be better spent on more bombs—isn't that what the Communists really understand?"

Such rhetorical questions imply their own negative answers. But there is nevertheless a positive answer. It is that educational and cultural activities are indeed making an important contribution toward ending the cold war on terms favorable to the interests of the United States and other democratic nations. To explain this answer one must begin by realizing that the cold war is not like a football game which can be won or lost some Saturday afternoon. It is more accurate to speak of liquidating the cold war than of winning it, and it is only common sense to recognize that this will be at best a slow process which must be pursued persistently on many fronts with great patience and effort.

Even though the cold war cannot be quickly and dramatically "won," it can, unfortunately, be quickly lost. This is the frustrating thing. It can be lost in Latin America by a rash of Castro-style revolutions, or in Southeast Asia by the crumbling of non-

Communist governments under the pressure of Communist aggression, or in Africa if the present non-Communist approach of the new nations there fails to achieve reasonably rapid progress.

To avert such disasters and to liquidate the cold war ultimately, four basic conditions must be met. The first essential, obviously, is to insure against any possible Communist military aggression by maintaining superior military strength which stands ready to defend the integrity of all independent nations. This requirement appears to have been met, at least for the moment, and will surely continue to receive priority. But this is only the beginning.

A second essential is for the community of advanced democratic nations to continue to grow in strength of every sort and to maintain an unswerving unity of purpose. This requires much more than heavy military expenditures and more than expanded trade. It requires a depth and breadth of mutual understanding, respect, and confidence among all these nations that will enable them to weather the stresses and strains of inevitable specific economic and political differences. Without such mutual understanding there can be no real community, and without a strong community there can be no security for the democratic world.

This essential mutual understanding between the United States and its democratic allies cannot be taken for granted. It must be steadily nurtured by a broad and fruitful interchange, at all levels, of intellectual, scientific and cultural activity. In the last analysis, it is this interchange which is the lifeblood of the democratic community, and always has been.

The extensive educational and cultural exchanges within the community of advanced democracies since the war—to which the United States has given major leadership through the Fulbright Act, the Smith-Mundt Act, and in other ways—have contributed much to building mutual understanding and unity. Although governmental programs may be but a minor part of a much larger whole, as was pointed out in the case of France, they have had a real influence. The examples of Germany and Japan have already been cited, but there is much further evidence. The U.S. Ambassador to Belgium, for example, told the Gardner Commission that he ranked the exchange program on a parity of importance with military assistance because of its value in promoting Belgian understanding of U.S. policies in matters such as the Congo, NATO defense, and the future of Europe. An American observer in Sweden said the exchange program's chief value is in "inspiring confidence in the United States as a political force in the world by providing evidence that the United States has a serious culture, that its civilization is not merely materialistic, is not superficial and immature, but has its roots firmly embedded in the best traditions of Western civilization." Such understanding is of greatest importance, he noted, in a country where scholars are so deeply involved in policy-making.

A third essential for liquidating the cold war is that the developing nations of Asia, Africa, and Latin America make steady and substantial progress toward their social and economic goals, within a framework of genuine national independence. The prime requirement for such progress is the development of each nation's educational and human resources and the building of strong institutions. And if the West is to help in that cause, it is vital that the developing nations acquire a deep and honest understanding of the United States and its policies and of the other democratic nations as well. Only then can they overcome fixed ideas on imperialism and colonialism and see clearly where their own interests lie; only then can they see the cold war not as a quarrel between two equally fearsome giants, but as a conflict between two very different ways of life in whose outcome they have a profound stake.

The illustrative cases cited earlier, such as India, Indonesia, and the African nations, demonstrate that the educational component of U.S. foreign policy has already achieved substantial gains both in helping the developing countries make progress toward their goals and in deepening the vitally needed understanding—in both directions—between them and the United States.

A fourth basic requirement for liquidating the cold war, and the most fundamental of all, is that the Soviet Union and Communist China relinquish once and for all their oft-repeated aim of world conquest by communism, and abandon the subversive strategies and tactics that go with this aim. Until this crucial change comes about, until the leading Communist nations genuinely accept "peaceful coexistence" not simply as a temporary expedient but as a paramount long-range goal, and until they are satisfied to concentrate upon their own internal development and leave others free to choose their way of life, the cold war will surely persist, with all its wastes and gruesome hazards. Such a fundamental change in the aims and strategies of the two great Communist powers will obviously require far-reaching changes within their own societies, along with the assurance that they, too, will be left free to pursue their way of life.

It would be naïve to expect these changes within the Communist nations to occur overnight, even though they are in heated dispute with each other. At best it is likely to be a slow evolutionary process geared to the gradual waning of initial revolutionary fervor and to a growing insistence by the Russian and Chinese peoples that they be given a better life. It is in the interest of the democratic nations to encourage and accelerate this evolutionary process.

Tentatively at least, there is cause for encouragement in the growing evidence of change within the Soviet Union, in the altered behavior of the Soviet government in international affairs, and in the eased relations with the West. The broadened educational and cultural interchange between the Soviet Union and the West has certainly been a reflection of this lessening of tensions and the mutual search for accommodation on certain previously unsettled questions. It may also have been a factor contributing to these changes, for cause and effect are not easy to disentangle once such a process is in train.

It is too soon, of course, for any definitive evaluation of the broadened interchange, but at this stage the prognosis is favorable. At the very least, it has helped destroy some mischievous misconceptions on both sides. Thousands of Soviet citizens, to cite one small example, having enjoyed with wild enthusiasm the University of Michigan Symphonic Band and having met personally its attractive and well-behaved members, will not be easily persuaded by any amount of future propaganda that all American youth are juvenile delinquents. By the same token, thousands of Americans have discovered from the Moiseyev Ballet and similar visitors that the Russian people under communism are still a highly artistic and also a friendly and very human people.

But these exchanges have had a deeper impact. They have given a considerable number of influential intellectuals in both countries a much better understanding not only of the real facts of life, but also of the substantial areas of mutual interest which they, as professionals, and their nations have. Though this does not eliminate the very serious national differences which still persist, it puts them in healthier and safer perspective.

"Large numbers of Polish leaders, specialists, and scholars," a well-informed American observer wrote to the Gardner Commission, ". . . have returned with their Communist-provided stereotypes shattered." The same surely can be said of many Soviet visitors, for they are human, too. This is not to say, of course, that these visitors have abondoned their loyalty to communism. But it does mean in many cases that they have returned home with a less rigid and doctrinaire view of the world, which is likely to be reflected in the influence they exert in their own circles at home and perhaps ultimately upon public policy.

This is not to say, either, that these exchanges are the panacea for ending the cold war; they clearly are not. Because they represent one of the few means by which the West can get through to the peoples of the Communist states and possibly influence the conduct of their governments, we may tend to overestimate what cultural relations as an arm of foreign policy can do. Nevertheless, there is strong reason to consider them one of the essential elements of an eventual solution, and an investment of very high yield.

* * *

Summing up, then, it is evident that what I have called the educational component has contributed substantially to the major objectives of U.S. foreign policy in the postwar period, including the objective of ending the cold war on terms compatible with the values and interests of American society.

It is also clear, however, that this contribution could have been, and could be today, considerably greater. The gap between opportunity and performance is explained largely by our failure to see the vital connection between educational and cultural activities and the basic aims of U.S. foreign policy. Many of our policy makers and legislators, and indeed most of us, have thought of these activities as unobjectionable or even good in themselves but only vaguely related to the nation's major aims and interests. Therefore, we have been inclined to treat them as side effects, as semi-luxuries, which could be expanded or contracted at will and administered in haphazard fashion, without serious consequences.

The time has come to see them for what they really are, to take them more seriously, and to exploit more fully the opportunity they provide. This leads us then to our final question: What practical steps can now be taken to strengthen this whole new dimension of U.S. foreign policy?

Chapter VI

Where Should We Go from Here?

Several considerations argue overwhelmingly for strengthening the educational component of U.S. foreign policy: its proven record of accomplishment; the great force of ideas, knowledge, and people in shaping world events; the gravity of America's international problems, commitments, and obligations; and the evident impossibility of handling these solely by political, economic and military means. How, then, can it best be strengthened? What specific policies should be pursued, what concrete steps taken, and who should take them? A brief summary of our thesis and findings may point to some answers.

The thesis, in a nutshell, stoutly denies that educational and cultural activities are a mere mishmash of "do good" endeavors which can contribute little or nothing to the conduct and success of U.S. foreign policy. They comprise, on the contrary, potent and timely measures—a fourth dimension of foreign policy—that can bolster the political, economic and military elements, grasp opportunities beyond their reach, and add much-needed flexibility, breadth, and depth. In short, this fourth dimension should be given parity of importance with the other three. As things stand today it has been underestimated, neglected, and often misunderstood.

We have already seen in the preceding chapters that educational and cultural factors have contributed to the foreign policy objectives that are essential to ending the cold war on acceptable terms—objectives that happily coincide with the long-term interests of many other nations. Further progress in that direction is dependent on the fulfillment of two other requirements basically educational in nature. One is to achieve a deeper understanding of the United States by other peoples so that they will comprehend better and more sympathetically the policies and actions of this nation in exercising its leadership in the common interest. The other is to provide Americans with a deeper understanding of the rest of the world so that American policies and actions, both public and private, will be well conceived and supported and thus more effective.

To do their proper job in the future, educational policies and measures must be shaped into a coherent whole by a clearer set of objectives, better planning, and more forceful and imaginative administration. They must enjoy greater political and financial support. They must be based on a strong partnership between government and the private sector. And they must have sufficient flexibility to be accommodated to the vicissitudes of over-all policy. Fortunately this nation possesses abundant resources in its people and institutions to build a much stronger educational component of foreign policy. Our reserves have been only fractionally utilized. To tap them more fully and apply them more efficiently is now the essential task.

Improving the Organization

Organization and administration may be less important than the substance of policy, but their improvement is an essential first step. Here the central issue is whether it will suffice to patch up the old machinery or whether a drastic overhaul is required. I find myself (having taken the opposite position while in Washington) forced reluctantly to the conclusion that without a major realignment in the present set-up there is no hope for achieving a strong and truly unified educational effort. Space does not permit arguing the case fully here, but a brief look at some of the inherent contradictions in the existing situation will suggest the grounds for my conclusion.

One can begin with AID, which has far more resources potentially available for promoting educational development than all other agencies combined. Its efforts must obviously be meshed with theirs, but who should direct whom? The plain truth is that AID cannot be directed from the outside, in Washington or overseas; many good men have tried it over the years and failed. This is nobody's fault; it is just the way a big complex foreign aid agency is. The logical answer, then, would seem to be for AID, as the power center of U.S. programs in developing countries, to coordinate the other agencies or absorb their functions. The difficulty here, however, is that AID already has more than it can handle just trying to coordinate itself. No one is effectively in charge of educational aid policy and strategy. Those who handle it, who actually have their hand on the throttle, find it difficult to collaborate with other agencies, as anxious as they often are to do so. Subject to too many who can overrule them and having no clear-cut policies, they can never be sure of being able to deliver on agreements reached.

Turn now to CU and USIA, which along with AID handle the main core of educational and cultural activities. CU, as we have seen, is severely handicapped: first, because its appropriation is an integral part—and perennially a major compromise area—of the State Department's over-all appropriation; second, because administratively it is strait-jacketed by State's ill-fitting rules and procedures; and third, because the world-wide exchange program for which it is responsible is actually managed in the field, where it really counts, by another agency, USIA. The Assistant Secretary of State who directs CU's operations is supposed, at the same time, to dispense policy guidance and even-handed justice to all agencies in this field, including USIA. His dilemma, of course, which never really gets resolved, is how to be both a party at interest and an impartial arbiter in cases complicated by long-standing bureaucratic rivalries.

USIA in some respects has the worst predicament of all—a split personality. It is first and foremost an information agency, managed by people skilled in journalism, schooled in the "psychological approach," and goaded constantly by certain Congressmen to pursue a "hard-sell" line. The first claim on USIA's budget and top managers is the latest crisis and each day's news. In handling this it is highly proficient. But at the same time USIA must also handle educational and cultural operations overseas—its own commingled with CU's—through a cultural affairs officer who is often torn between two Washington bosses with apparently conflicting approaches, and who is subordinate to a public affairs officer whose first concern must be with USIA's information mission. If he is really well-qualified in his field of educational and cultural affairs and not just an information specialist awaiting his turn as a public affairs officer, he is inevitably whip-sawed by these incompatibilities.

Seasoned career people in USIA defend this marriage of responsibilities on the plausible grounds that information and educational and cultural affairs are essentially the same thing arrayed along a spectrum from short run to long. To do an effective job of supporting U.S. foreign policy, they argue, USIA and each embassy's chief public affairs officer must have both sets of "tools" in hand. The implication is that in other hands the cultural "tools" would be misused by not being oriented toward supporting foreign policy objectives. Though fully respecting the sincerity of the case, I have trouble accepting its validity after having observed the operation both at home and overseas. Despite having much in common, information activities and educational and cultural activities are in practice very different things—or at least should be. The very working language of USIA—aiming at "target audiences," getting "the message" across, "the low-key treatment," and the like—suggests the distinction between the two and their incompatibility.

The "information approach" is essentially a one-way process, legitimately preoccupied with developing sympathetic foreign attitudes toward U.S. policies and actions. Day by day it endeavors to explain these policies and actions and to put them in the best light that truth affords. It is also a competitive process, daily occupied with exposing and criticizing policies and propaganda that are hostile to the United States. The "educational and cultural approach" on the other hand, is also concerned with developing honest and sympathetic understanding, but it is a two-way process, calculated to foster *mutual* understanding and to benefit both parties to the exchange. It is not concerned with day-to-day events or with explaining and justifying specific and immediate U.S. policies and actions; its main concern is with the deeper currents that affect relations between peoples and with the broader and more basic U.S. foreign policy goals. Ambassador George Allen, who once headed the USIA, said he never had any problem distinguishing the two when he was serving abroad as ambassador—he always knew which staff member to call if he had an information problem and which to call about an educational or cultural question.

It is the various incongruities in the present situation—and not any criticism of the people or organizations involved—which force me to conclude that a basic realignment is needed. It would be foolish, of course, to assume that there can be a perfect solution to any organizational problem as complex as this one. The aim must be to find a solution which combines the most advantages with the fewest disadvantages. Some would argue, and with considerable persuasion, that the balance of advantage lies with leaving well enough alone, because any major reorganization is inevitably accompanied by pain, confusion, and uncertainty. But well enough in this case is simply not good enough. If a reorganization of the sort suggested below is well thought through, carefully planned in advance, and not undertaken too precipitately, these hazards can be much reduced.

The first requirement, I submit, if we are really serious about achieving a strong and unified educational component of foreign policy, is for someone to be put in charge and given clear enough responsibility and authority to get the job done. For this purpose I suggest that there be created within the Department of State a new position of under-secretary rank, one which was, in fact, envisaged by the original Fulbright-Hays Bill. The new under-secretary would be charged with developing a unified set of policies to guide *all* international activities of the government in this field and ensuring their proper coordination. He would include within his purview, among other things, the present confusing clutter of international scientific activities of the federal government, which today tend to be treated separately from the rest but which in reality are largely—or should be—an integral part of educational and cultural affairs.

The second requirement is to find a way to combine under one roof and one direction enough of the central elements to insure that policies and actions can be jointly planned and operationally meshed, both in Washington and in the field. Here the solution which strikes me as most promising is to create within the State Department and under the authority of the new undersecretary a semi-independent U.S. International Education Agency (or Foundation)—having much the same status within State that AID now has—which would amalgamate the principal educational and cultural activities now in the hands of CU (which would disappear), USIA, and AID, both in Washington and abroad. Its orientation would not be set by any one of the competing philosophies that have characterized those three organizations but by a synthesis of the best elements of all three, and therefore more comprehensive, flexible, and consistent. It would seek a separate appropriation under the Fulbright-Hays Act and also administer that portion of foreign aid funds applying to educational development.

The key to the new agency's success, of course, would be the quality of its staff. First consideration should be given to absorbing the ablest people now working on educational and cultural matters in the present agencies (whose jobs would be abolished by this move). Their experience and their dedication would be indispensable to the new agency's success. But it should also have ample latitude to recruit fresh, competent talent, particularly from the educational, cultural, and philanthropic fields, and to build the strongest possible professional corps. In this effort the new agency would undoubtedly enjoy the full cooperation of the academic and cultural community.

Its overseas branches—perhaps designated U.S. Education Foundations—would similarly consolidate exchange activities, libraries, educational development, and similar functions now divided between USIA and AID abroad. Both in the advanced countries where AID does not function and in the developing countries where it does, the USIA would continue to function, but now as a specialized information agency unencumbered by educational and cultural activities.

The director of each overseas branch of the consolidated educational and cultural agency, who would be of ministerial rank at the larger embassies, would replace the present cultural affairs officer and would report directly to the ambassador. Besides directing the operations of his own organization, he would seek to harmonize the related activities of all U.S. government agencies, and he would also be the main point of contact and cooperation with private U.S. organizations functioning within that country. For the first time, in short, there would be a high officer in each U.S. mission specifically responsible for maintaining a comprehensive view of all U.S. educational and cultural activities in a country, in the light of the special circumstances of that country and of U.S. foreign policy objectives there. Then and only then would it become possible to have a truly integrated "country plan."

This suggestion may well give rise to legitimate cautions, doubts, and criticisms which will merit serious study. One objection may be that the information program would be weakened by losing control over educational and cultural activities. My opinion is that quite the opposite would happen. Another criticism might be that taking educational development functions from AID might lead to fragmentation of the aid program. This is a more serious objection, but it is my impression that in most aid missions even now educational matters are in fact quite segregated from the rest of the program and distressingly on their own. No existing unity would be destroyed, but a new one might be created. A stronger hand and clearer sense of strategy is much needed in AID's approach to educational development in most countries.

What is perhaps the most important advantage of the suggested arrangement is its probable salutary impact on American education itself and on our other cultural institutions. By providing a more central and visible point of contact and cooperation between government and the private sector—and hopefully also a more sophisticated understanding of the unique nature and functions of our own educational and cultural institutions—

this new agency could contribute much to strengthening them while at the same time mobilizing their great potential for contributing to the nation's foreign relations and its long-range foreign policy objectives.

Turning now from the issue of organization, let us consider what policies would be appropriate to different groups of countries and to such central issues as purpose, quality, efficiency, and finance.

Policies Toward Western Europe and Japan

The strong trend at present toward retrenching U.S. educational and cultural activities in the Atlantic community and Japan reflects a dangerously short-sighted view. We should have learned by now not to take our friends for granted, and to invest as adequately in long-run relationships as in solutions to immediate problems. The long-run success of American foreign policy, and the security and welfare of the United States, are obviously very dependent upon our relations with these nations. Most of them are currently undergoing profound social, economic and political changes whose consequences cannot now be foreseen. New generations with different attitudes and conceptions of the world and of the United States are moving into positions of power and leadership in Europe and Japan. The United States itself is changing, in ways that belie old stereotypes. As a result there is probably less genuine understanding and less sense of mutual interest between the United States and Europe today than shortly after the war. And it would certainly be imprudent to assume that the greatly improved postwar understanding between the United States and the older generation in Japan applies equally to the restless younger generation there. What is done today under these changing conditions to insure continuing mutual understanding between Europe, Japan, and the United States can affect profoundly the degree of unity and cooperation we will enjoy a decade from now. In a period when the NATO alliance may be under increasing strain, it will be all the more necessary that the basic understanding among the peoples of the

West be deepened and that it temper the differences and disagreements that arise between governments.

A further good reason to continue strong educational and cultural efforts in Western Europe is that there—especially in France and England, but in other countries too—the basic attitudes toward the United States of many future Asian and African leaders are now being formed. Effort wisely spent today within a one-mile radius of the Sorbonne or the University of London could well have as profound an impact on future U.S. relations with Africa and Asia as equal effort spent within those regions themselves.

All this does not mean that U.S. educational and cultural programs in Europe and Japan should remain frozen in their present pattern. On the contrary, there is evident need for a thorough-going reappraisal (as the example of France, cited in the preceding chapter, suggests). With Europe, of course, the mainstream of cultural relations will continue to flow outside governmental channels. But official initiative and stimulation will remain essential, and here several new emphases and innovations merit consideration: first, a more vigorous effort to strengthen the dialogue between the American, and the European and Japanese university communities and with the younger scholars, writers, artists, journalists, labor leaders, and politicians of these nations; second, support of new types of multinational institutions in such fields as educational and scientific research, advanced graduate training, and the arts, where able scholars and young talent from various countries could work together for sustained periods (as scientists now do at the European Organization for Nuclear Research in Geneva); third, the creation of new forms of cooperation among advanced countries in their approaches to developing countries. For example, France, the United Kingdom, and the United States might collaborate in teaching French in English-speaking Africa and English in French-speaking Africa, so that the new African nations could communicate better with each other and with a wider range of advanced countries. As another example, various Western European nations might join forces with the United States in helping Latin American nations develop stronger educational systems and cultural institutions. By tying together bilateral programs where possible, as well as by strengthening UNESCO and other international agencies, their combined effectiveness could be increased and the sharp edge of competing nationalisms blunted, to the benefit of all.

Policies Toward Developing Countries

Hopefully the next decade will see heartening progress in all the nations of Asia, Africa, the Middle East, and Latin America. But in many of them it will surely also witness extensive turmoil and disappointment. The road to national development and maturity, requiring as it does the uprooting of old cultural patterns and power structures, is bound to be a rough and precarious one (as our own history demonstrates). Headlines can be expected to blazon repeated alarms and excursions as internal struggles occur, as old governments topple and new ones replace them, and as each in turn tries courting first one outside power and then another, playing both ends against the middle. The painful upheavals of recent years in Cuba and the Congo, Cyprus and Central America, Viet-Nam and Laos were only the curtain-raiser for an action-packed drama yet to be played. As the United States, like it or not, will be involved in virtually every scene of the drama, we will be well advised to maintain a long view, a cool head, and an abundance of patience toward this turbulent process.

Shifting circumstances will require a high flexibility of short-range policies and tactics, but their effectiveness will depend heavily upon whatever underlying strengths have been built by positive long-range policies, consistently applied despite the inevitable ups-and-downs of political conditions. One of the most basic and rewarding of these policies is to help these nations develop their people and institutions. It is a long and arduous process, but it is also a process to which the United States can perhaps contribute even more than to economic development by itself. Nothing could be more essential to their progress and maturity, or to building friendly and fruitful relations with them.

Our primary attention should focus on the "movers and shap-

ers" of the new countries, on educational development broadly
defined, and on the fostering of cultural, political and social institutions. One of the advantages would be to leaven any ex-
cessively materialistic emphasis of U.S. aid and thereby demonstrate that the American people care deeply about cultural and
humanistic values as well. It would also help rectify the imbalance of emphasis in U.S. foreign policy between short-term and
long-term considerations.

The Leaders and Shapers of Change

The Gardner Commission wisely emphasized that in selecting
foreign participants for exchange programs, special effort should
be made "to seek out and select those candidates . . . who are
sufficiently vigorous and restless to help promote desirable social
and economic change." In practice, the Commission pointed out,
this will mean greater emphasis on "rising young adults, including some who are locally considered 'radical,' 'left-wing,' or politically dissident." Exchange programs should likewise include,
the Commission urged, a good proportion of "have-nots"—able
people capable of rising from the lower echelons of their society—so that in keeping with this nation's traditions, "an American exchange experience never becomes a privilege restricted to
the elite."[1]

Paying special attention to the movers and shapers of change
in the developing countries, just as in the more developed ones,
requires giving emphasis to exchanges of youth leaders, young
intellectuals, labor leaders, women leaders, and rising young politicians and government officials. It should be remembered that
in most countries, more than is apparent in our own, intellectuals carry great influence in public affairs.

To implement the foregoing policies will require a lowering of
the English language barrier which now automatically excludes
many of the most talented "have-nots" from an opportunity to
study in the United States. This means investing more in special

[1] U.S. Advisory Commission on International Educational and Cultural
Affairs, *A Beacon of Hope—The Exchange-of-Persons Program* (Washington:
GPO, 1963), p. 4.

programs of English language instruction for prospective foreign students and other visitors to the United States. To reduce another kind of barrier a flexible and realistic visa policy is required which will permit potential leaders of other societies—including some who may be our vocal critics—an honest, first-hand encounter with American life. To admit into the United States only the agreeable visitors, only those who are or profess to be our friends, and only those who have never fought a cause under a radical banner, is to pursue an illusory security and comfort.

Educational Development

A larger proportion of U.S. aid funds should, in many recipient countries, be directed toward the development of education and human resources. But it is obviously not enough merely to spend more money on education; what is even more important is to spend it on the right things and in the right ways. This calls for a more comprehensive view and a clearer strategy of educational development than now exists on the part of the Americans concerned as well as in the recipient countries. It requires a larger supply of good "educational strategists," competent to take a broad view and to design and pursue a more rational and efficient course of educational development, integrated with the requirements of social and economic growth. The new nations must be provided with more and better technical help to evolve educational plans, but these should reflect primarily their own determination of needs and priorities, not the preconceptions of visiting advisers.

The best strategy of educational aid is one concerned not only with helping developing countries expand their educational systems but also with helping them change those systems to fit their needs and resources. The United States, after a decade of unprecedented innovation and improvement in its own educational system, is well equipped to assist them in reforming and improving theirs through research, experimentation, and innovation. Without far-reaching educational reforms—of structure, curriculum, and methods—these countries will fail to achieve the educational results they desperately need. This does not mean, of course, simply exporting American educational models which, like the European, are often inappropriate and too expensive. There must be a premium on invention and adaptation which will tailor the educational systems of the developing countries to their own circumstances.

To build and staff their own educational institutions and to meet other pressing needs for trained people, these countries will for some time to come have to send some of their best talent to be educated abroad. There is great opportunity to raise the value of the contribution they can make by improving the selection process, by planning better their overseas training and increasing its usefulness to them, and by making sure that on their return home they get into employment where their newly acquired knowledge can be used to best advantage. All these improvements call for close cooperation between the sending and receiving countries and fresh inventiveness on both ends. The private sector, with the U.S. government in close collaboration, could do much more along these lines.

Cultural Development

For a new nation to achieve national unity, stability, and maturity, it must develop a confidence and self-respect based on pride in its cultural heritage and its present accomplishments. Economic growth and technical modernization alone cannot provide this; indeed, their initial effect is to uproot the very cultural patterns and value systems that previously provided the foundation for social stability and individual security. Unless strong new cultural patterns and value systems emerge, the society in transition can disintegrate. Unhappily this is a process about which even the wisest are still ignorant.

It is evident, however, that each society must evolve its own cultural patterns, values, and institutions. Other societies can undoubtedly help, even though it is a subtle and delicate affair, often best dealt with through private channels. It would be well, nevertheless, for our governmental efforts also to pay more heed to this fundamental matter, which thus far has been too much ignored. There is no lack of useful things to do, most of them modest in cost but potentially very effective. New societies could be helped, for example, to create their own libraries, theaters, dance and musical groups, museums, art galleries, and archives to preserve the fugitive evidence of their national history. Through technical assistance in historical research, archeology, and musicology they can be helped to discover their past. They can likewise be helped to enrich their current artistic and literary creativity.

The United States should also increase its efforts to help emerging nations establish their own book publishing and distribution facilities, building on the splendid start already made by Franklin Publications, the Ford Foundation, and USIA. With radio and television facilities mushrooming throughout the developing regions, it is urgent that more be done to encourage their use for raising educational and cultural levels on a massive scale. U.S. educational and commercial broadcasters could both do much to help in this respect.

Cultural development also requires language development and literacy. But before literacy programs can even be undertaken in many areas, the indigenous languages must first acquire a written form. Moreover, all developing countries must have a second language, if not a third, in order to tap the world's storehouse of technical and other knowledge, to trade in world markets and conduct diplomacy, to communicate with their neighbors (as in Africa) or even with themselves (as in India). A greatly increased effort is necessary all around the world to satisfy the burgeoning demand for learning English. In all these aspects of over-all development, the United States has a role to play which should strengthen international linkages and foster friendly relations between the advanced and emerging nations.

Policies Toward Communist Countries

There are compelling reasons why the United States should seize every reasonable opportunity to expand cultural interchange with Communist countries, and to shield such exchanges, so far as possible, against the inevitable fluctuations of political climate and tensions. One of the greatest threats to peace today is the self-imposed isolation of the Communist societies, which on both sides breeds dangerous distortions and miscalculations. Cultural interchange is one of the best ways to reduce this threat and to nourish liberalizing tendencies within the Communist countries. The progressive opening of the curtain since the death of Stalin and the evident desire of Eastern European countries to expand their cultural intercourse with the West is a heartening development from which both sides stand to benefit—but probably most of all the open democratic societies.

The U.S.–U.S.S.R. exchange program of recent years, though not without many problems, has established a sufficiently encouraging record to warrant further expansion. Difficulties will remain, of course, so long as the Soviet Union is not prepared to give American scholars and experts the same full measure of freedom of inquiry and research that theirs are given in the United States. This is a point, of course, on which we cannot expect full satisfaction so long as the Soviet system is what it is, but we can press for improvement in the situation. These and other irritants should not discourage a still greater effort. Some of the problems, particularly those which apparently are more the result of bureaucracy than of politics, might be ironed out if special efforts were made outside the framework of official negotiations. It might be a useful experiment, for example, to ask an *ad hoc* committee of leading American and Soviet academicians to investigate the complaints on either side concerning academic exchanges and to recommend practical ways for overcoming them.

The United States should continue to press for the enlarged exchange and open sale of newspapers, periodicals and books in the U.S.S.R. and for more interchange of TV and radio programs and films. Only in this way can substantial numbers of the people in one country get better acquainted with the other. The opening of windows to the free world cannot be without some effect on Soviet society, even if it is only to encourage currents of thought and of change already present there which tend toward moderation. It is hard to see how all the various contacts that have taken place since Stalin's death can bring anything but advantage to the United States and the West generally, so long as they do not induce any false hopes and conceptions about Soviet policy.

The time seems ripe to expand cultural exchanges with other Communist countries of Eastern Europe, especially Poland, Czechoslovakia, Hungary, and Rumania. Those nations have strong historic ties with Western Europe. Everything that can be done through communication and cultural relations to restore and strengthen those ties ought to be done. It is true that in carrying on exchanges with Eastern Europe we have to deal with and through unrepresentative Communist regimes, but the important point is that these programs reach the people.

Communist China, of course, is a special case. But the same factors that argue for withholding diplomatic recognition argue equally for initiating cultural communication. Since officially sponsored exchanges are not currently feasible, the U.S. government should encourage—or at least not discourage—experimental efforts to establish such a dialogue through private channels. Perhaps Chinese Communist authorities would oppose it, but the effort would be well worth making. The longer that mainland China remains out of intellectual communication with the West, and especially the United States, the more serious the consequences are likely to be.

The Policy of Quality First

There are innumerable instances of superb quality in the past record of America's educational and cultural activities abroad. The evidence is clear that investment in quality yields extra dividends out of all proportion to the extra costs. It is equally clear that shoddiness, mediocrity, and niggardliness in this area of foreign policy are worse than wasteful; they can be downright counterproductive. Priority should therefore be given to raising the quality of existing programs, even if necessary at the cost of reducing their size.

There are many specific and rather obvious ways to raise standards all along the line at very modest cost. For example, the quality of American academic personnel and specialists sent overseas for extended periods could be improved by raising stipends to more realistic levels, by providing travel allowances for wives, by relaxing rigid scheduling rules in order better to accommodate the demands on busy people, and by a more positive effort to recruit the nation's best talent with the help of professional societies, foundations, and other knowledgeable groups.

The effectiveness of educational development assistance could be enhanced by bringing competent university personnel into the planning of projects at an early stage, by putting more effort into practical research and the evaluation of projects in order to develop useful knowledge about the educational development process. Most helpful of all would be the recruitment and intensive training of a small cadre of first-rate "educational development strategists" to serve in the aid program.

The quality of American cultural representation abroad could be improved by an intensive effort to recruit persons who are themselves creative, as well as being well-versed in the educational and cultural aspects of American life, to serve as resident scholars, writers, or artists in an appropriate embassy for a year or two. Career cultural representatives should periodically be returned to American campuses and other centers in the mainstream of American cultural life for their own intellectual refreshment. The important thing is that the leaders of intellectual life in foreign countries really be brought into contact with the sources and the living representatives of Amerian culture and not just with government functionaries bearing the label of cultural affairs officers.

Even some relatively minor administrative changes could bring rich rewards. The effectiveness of visits by foreign leaders and specialists could be increased by raising the quality of escort-interpreter services. More time should be devoted to arranging visitors' itineraries well in advance, getting them to see people and places off the well-worn paths, and slowing down their hectic pace. The cultural presentations program could be improved in a variety of ways, but especially by not overscheduling the performing artists who go abroad. They should be allowed to stay in one place long enough to catch their breath and to leave a deeper impression. Foreign student programs would benefit from an overseas system of selection and guidance run in behalf of

American colleges and universities, more English language instruction and general orientation for newly arrived students, better advisory and other services for them on campuses, and greater effort to keep in touch with "alumni" after their return to their own countries.

The legislative authority already exists for most of these improvements and many others, but several practical obstacles must be removed. The biggest obstacle is the unwillingness of congressional appropriations committees to see funds spent for most of these purposes. Their propensity to judge educational and cultural programs by the size of the numbers involved and the smallness of the unit costs has in numerous cases encouraged an actual decline in quality. Another impediment is the propensity of the administering bureaucracies to retreat into the illusory sanctuary of routine rules and procedures, which rob such activities of their flexibility and often of their quality and effectiveness. Their further tendency is to avoid a critical evaluation of past experience, where the most useful lessons for the future are to be found. If these various deadening influences could be overcome, a rapid and substantial increase in quality could be achieved at surprisingly little cost.

Strengthening Government-Private Cooperation

The extraordinary dependence of the educational and cultural dimension of foreign policy upon private initiative and support, which has been stressed throughout this book, makes it imperative that government and the private sector work in close harmony and that their respective roles be as clearly defined as possible. This is no easy matter in a pluralistic society where the freedom of scholarship, religion, and the arts from government interference is highly valued and jealously guarded, and where the duties of the federal government even with respect to domestic education and cultural life are still anything but clear.

Ideological and constitutional debates on these matters have been singularly unproductive. A more rewarding approach toward clarifying the division of labor is to begin by recognizing, very pragmatically, that some things which should be done, only government can do; other things only the private sector can do or can do much better; while still other things require a combined effort.

Thus, for example, it takes the federal government to reach a general exchange agreement with the Soviet Union, to establish and sustain a well-functioning network of binational fellowship commissions abroad, or to maintain an expensive system of overseas libraries. But only the private sector can actually carry the strengths and vitality of American education and culture abroad, or provide education to foreign students, or produce books which portray to others the character and accomplishments of American society. Because they enjoy a freedom of action and a relative immunity from criticism and constraint, universities, foundations, and private organizations can take initiatives and establish working relationships abroad beyond the practical scope of government. Some of the foregoing private functions can only be done on an adequate scale with a measure of federal financial support.

With these facts of life in mind, it is possible to suggest the following three basic roles for government. First, it should help remove roadblocks to a free international trade in ideas and knowledge, and encourage the private sector to engage vigorously in such trade. Second, it should keep the private sector well informed. For, if the private sector knows what the government considers to be important, useful, or harmful, knows what the government itself is doing and where it is heading, then it can usually be counted on to respond cooperatively and intelligently. But when it lacks such knowledge and perspective, the private sector, like the government, becomes confused and less effective. Third, whenever the success of foreign policy objectives calls for certain actions which the private sector cannot reasonably be expected to undertake on its own, the federal government should take the initiative and do the necessary. Sometimes government must act alone, but in many cases the best solution lies in a partnership under which the federal government provides policy guidance and financial support and private organizations carry out the operations.

Beyond these three roles the government should provide general leadership, particularly by calling attention to important needs, by setting good standards, and by encouraging a more unified national effort (most of all by putting its own house in order). But leadership here is not the monopoly of government. It must come also from private individuals and institutions in the form of imaginative initiatives and pilot experiments which can pave the way for government itself, and of critical appraisals and positive proposals to improve the national effort, both public and private.

Within the frame of this very general definition of government's role, a few more specific guides may be suggested. First, government agencies should try even harder to harness the energies and capacities of private agencies rather than try to do everything themselves. Universities, for example, should be given larger responsibilities under the aid program, as already suggested. Professional societies, to take another example, should be asked to insure good U.S. representation at important international meetings of experts—often under nongovernmental auspices—and should be given financial assistance where necessary to achieve this purpose. But where the government does call on private agencies to do a job, partially financed by government, it should pay as much attention thereafter to auditing the quality of performance as it now devotes to auditing the books.

Second, when a government agency contracts with a private one to render a service (with a university, let us say, to manage a teacher-training project in Afghanistan, or the Governmental Affairs Institute to handle some visiting foreign experts), the private agency should be brought into the planning process at the earliest possible stage, not only to tap its professional competence but to insure that the final project is well suited to its strengths and proper functions. There is no historic precedent for such an intensive use of our universities in foreign relations as exists today. Unless government contract officers understand the nature and aims of the university—and unless academic people appreciate the nature of government and its problems—this relationship is bound to turn sour. Much has been done to clarify it, but more still is needed.

Third, government officers should understand the unique

functions and capabilities of private foundations and not view them simply as a pot of money to be tapped if possible whenever government funds for a particular purpose are low. Foundations, while preserving their independence, can occasionally be helpful to government by doing things beyond government's own capabilities. But they should not be asked to assume government's own proper responsibilities, as they were, for instance, a few years ago when a government officer pushed the panic button and pressured foundations to provide help for the influx of Cuban refugees, of the sort which government itself should have supplied and soon did.

Fourth, government agencies, most notably the intelligence agencies, should avoid asking private organizations and scholars to do things which might compromise their integrity or jeopardize their future effectiveness. Fear that Congress might not approve the use of regular funds for certain legitimate and important purposes—such as a research project by a group of scholars—makes it tempting to use unaccountable funds for the purpose, which automatically lends an air of intrigue and secrecy to an enterprise that by right should be in the open.

Fifth, the government should speak up forthrightly when certain private activities in the international field are clearly jeopardizing, however unintentionally, the nation's best interests. An example might be the export of certain commercial movies that are obviously creating a distorted and derogatory impression of this nation which is harmful to its foreign relations. This is obviously a more difficult problem for government to handle, however, than control or prohibition of certain exports to Russia, Cuba or China, where the national interest is also involved. The real issue here is not one of freedom of expression or of concealing honest but unpleasant facts about the United States. It is whether private profits should be placed above the nation's interests, simply because in this case the product happens to be a motion picture instead of a machine tool. Yet the problem is far more difficult because there is wide room for legitimate differences of opinion in each individual case, and the government can be wrong. Thus official censorship is certainly not the answer. Undoubtedly the best hope lies in plain talk and plain facts, such as Edward R. Murrow had the courage to use as Director of USIA, and in relying ultimately upon informed public opinion and businessmen's basic sense of public service.

Strengthening International Mechanisms of Cooperation

The United States should expand its already substantial leadership in promoting multilateral approaches in educational, scientific and cultural affairs—through the United Nations and its specialized agencies (especially UNESCO), through regional organizations such as the O.A.S. and the O.E.C.D., and through *ad hoc* cooperation among friendly nations.

The reasons are very practical. A purely bilateral approach to cultural relations has shortcomings as great as a purely bilateral approach to military security or international trade. Particularly in this field, where national sensitivities and suspicion of "cultural imperialism" run high, more can sometimes be accomplished—of high value to U.S. foreign policy objectives and to other nations as well—through channels not identified with the special interests of any one country. Moreover, as experience with the World Bank, the U.N. Special Fund, or the Development Assistance Committee of the O.E.C.D. has demonstrated, the United States can best encourage its friends to take a broader outlook and to accept a larger share of the responsibility by joining forces with them in multilateral undertakings. There is no doubt that American funds put through multilateral channels often yield substantially larger returns than the equivalent amount spent through our own national agencies—and the effects of the two methods can be highly complementary.

The tiny fraction of the U.S. government's total educational, scientific and cultural expenditure which now flows through multilateral agencies should be enlarged. But along with this, the U.S. government should make a strenuous effort to help improve the management, programs, and personnel of these agencies by paying closer attention to their day-to-day problems and inner workings and by making it more attractive and feasible for well-qualified Americans to serve on their staffs.

Financial Policies to Support an Adequate Effort

It was noted earlier that financial malnutrition, crippling restrictions in appropriation measures, and excessive reliance on foreign currencies have handicapped the quality, balance, flexibility, and effectiveness of the educational component of foreign policy. A further handicap has been the inability of operating agencies in most cases to make financial commitments beyond a single fiscal year, or to carry uncommitted funds from one year to the next. Existing legislation provides ample authority to solve most of these problems. Once again the practical solution lies in the appropriations process. The central question here, however, is how large the federal effort should be. Quite evidently it should be substantially greater, but no one now can say with assurance how much greater, especially since we do not know accurately how much is being spent right now on the entire educational side of foreign policy. The combined outlays of CU, USIA, and AID on these activities is on the order of $200 million, and to this must be added the smaller outlays of numerous other agencies. It seems safe to conclude in any event that the sum total being spent on the educational component of foreign policy is no more than one per cent of what is spent annually on the military component.

This comparison in itself, of course, proves little. But it does suggest that the U.S. economy and the federal budget could stand a substantial increase in educational and cultural activities without serious strain. It tends also to confirm the view that as a nation we have not taken this dimension of foreign policy nearly as seriously as others have.

The important point is that a sizable gap has developed over the years between the needs in this field and our actual performance, a gap which now needs urgently to be closed. What is required to close it is obviously something more than a trivial percentage increase each year. It will take a succession of larger increases which, in the course of five years or so, will roughly double the effort. Along with such budgetary increases, however, there must be a considerable strengthening of administrative machinery so that the quality and efficiency of the program can grow along with its size.

There is good reason to assume that bolder action by the government will stimulate a corresponding response by the private sector. The schools and colleges and universities, cultural institutions, and various specialized organizations all require greater support for their larger role in world affairs. Most of this additional support must come from the budgets of state and local governments and from private and corporate philanthropy. It is encouraging, therefore, to see the steady growth of concern and support for international educational and cultural affairs throughout the country.

A Final Word

There is no shortage of ideas about how to make educational, scientific and cultural activities a more vigorous aspect of U.S. foreign policy. But the reader who has patiently come this far may reasonably ask, "Well and good, I accept your line of argument and even most of your suggestions for future action, but what do you honestly believe are the prospects? Is there any reasonable chance to overcome the obstacles which thus far have made education and culture a stepchild of foreign policy?"

It is a fair and reasonable question, and my candid answer is this. It would be naïve to expect a sudden shift in attitudes and priorities or an overnight change of pace that would produce a burst of action along the lines suggested. These activities will keep growing, but they will undoubtedly continue to have an uphill struggle for years to come.

But there is this to be said on the optimistic side. Events are moving perhaps more rapidly than we realize. It is encouraging, for example, to note how many of the plans laid in 1961 and 1962 are already improving our cultural relations. The reason, I think, is clear enough: there is a quiet but broad support across the nation and throughout the world to make something more of the human side of international relations. There is a thrust of intuitive opinion, harbored by people of every station, that the time has come to add a new and more constructive dimension to foreign relations and foreign policy. The black headlines of crisis cannot rule us forever unchallenged. There must be something more that can be done by ordinary people, something not left to mere chance or solely in the hands of higher authorities.

I have no doubt that eventually—if the world can hold together—the educational component will take its place alongside the long-established ones. What has been suggested here and much more will come to pass. The real problem is how to speed up the advance, for the sooner it happens the sooner we can all sleep more easily.

Appendix Table 1

INTERNATIONAL EDUCATIONAL, SCIENTIFIC, AND CULTURAL ACTIVITIES OF U.S. AGENCIES PRIMARILY CONCERNED WITH FOREIGN AFFAIRS

Line		State Dept.	USIA	AID*	Defense Dept.	Peace Corps
	Exchange-of-Persons Programs					
1	U.S. students and faculty studying abroad	•	•			
2	Foreign students and faculty studying in U.S. institutions	•	•	•		
3	Special training programs in U.S. for foreign participants	•		•	•	
4	Services to foreign leaders and specialists on short-term visits to U.S.	•	•			
5	Short-term U.S. specialists abroad	•	•	•	•	•
6	Exchanges of scientific and technical personnel	•	•	•	•	•
7	U.S. technical assistance experts to developing countries		•	•	•	•
8	U.S. teachers and professors to teach in foreign institutions			•	•	•
9	Foreign teachers to teach in U.S. education	•			•	
10	Foreign student travel tours in U.S.	•				
11	Other foreign travel tours in U.S.	•		•	•	
12	Travel tours of U.S. groups abroad	•				
13	Training of foreign military personnel in U.S.				•	
14	Training of foreign military personnel overseas by U.S. personnel				•	
15	Training of U.S. military by foreign personnel					
16	Financial support of private exchange programs	•	•			
17	Facilitation of private exchanges	•	•			

Exchange of Educational Materials and Exhibitions

	18	19	20	21	22	23	24	25	26	27	28	29	30	31	32	33	34
18 Operation of U.S. Libraries and Cultural Centers abroad							•						•				
19 Distribution of U.S. books and publications abroad							•						•				
20 U.S. exhibits overseas: books, art, technical, trade fairs, etc.							•						•				
21 Overseas distribution of U.S. films, recordings, radio and TV programs							•						•				
22 Sending U.S. performing artists, athletes, entertainers overseas							•						•				
23 Encouraging flow of foreign exhibits, films, books, cultural presentations to U.S.							•						•				

Development Grants, Loans and Contracts for Educational Development

	18	19	20	21	22	23	24	25	26	27	28	29	30	31	32	33	34
24 To foreign governments for formal education								•	•	•	•	•	•	•	•	•	•
25 To foreign governments for specialized training institutions and programs																	
26 To U.S. schools, colleges, universities to improve foreign language instruction																	
27 To U.S. universities for instruction and research on foreign cultures																	
28 Textbooks and other teaching materials to foreign institutions																	
29 U.S. university contracts to assist foreign institutions																	

Promotion of Scientific and Scholarly Research and Exchange of Knowledge

	18	19	20	21	22	23	24	25	26	27	28	29	30	31	32	33	34
30 To strengthen research capabilities of foreign countries																	
31 Research activities abroad by U.S. and/or foreign personnel																	
32 Research and scientific training of foreigners in U.S.																	
33 Exchange of scientific and scholarly documents																	
34 U.S. participation in international scientific and scholarly meetings																	

Appendix Table 1 (cont.)

Line		State Dept.	USIA	AID*	Defense Dept.	Peace Corps	Line
35	Participation in cooperative international research projects	•		•	•		35
	Participation in Official International Organizations						
36	Helps formulate U.S. policies on international organizations	•	•	•	•	•	36
37	Represents U.S. government at international conferences	•	•	•	•	•	37
38	Programs international fellows in U.S.	•		•			38
39	Nominates Americans for international fellowships	•					39
	Special Programs						
40	Supports American studies in foreign institutions	•	•	•	•	•	40
41	Teaching English as a second language	•	•	•	•		41
42	Support of U.S.-sponsored schools and colleges abroad	•	•	•			42
43	Production of textbooks abroad			•			43

* Includes services rendered abroad for the State Department (CU).

Appendix Table 2
INTERNATIONAL EDUCATIONAL, SCIENTIFIC, AND CULTURAL ACTIVITIES OF U.S. AGENCIES PRIMARILY CONCERNED WITH DOMESTIC AFFAIRS

Note: Numbers Refer to the Activities Listed in Table 1

National Science Foundation, 1–6, 9, 16, 30–39

Department of Health, Education and Welfare:
    Office of Education, 1–4, 7–9, 17, 26–27, 31, 34–39
    National Institutes of Health, 1–4, 6, 17, 30–39
    Public Health Service, 3–4, 7, 31, 33–38
    Social Security Administration, 3–4, 38
    Children's Bureau, 3–4
    Office of Vocational Rehabilitation, 3–4, 38

National Aeronautics and Space Administration, 2–4, 6, 20, 32–37

Department of Agriculture, 3–4, 7, 17, 20, 31, 34, 36–38

Department of Commerce:
    Bureau of Census, 3–4, 7, 34–35
    Bureau of Public Roads, 3–4, 7, 35, 39
    Coast and Geodetic Survey, 3–4, 7, 34–35, 39
    Maritime Administration, 2–4, 7, 33, 35
    Bureau of Standards, 3–4, 6–7, 33
    Office of Technical Services, 31, 33–35, 37–39
    Weather Bureau, 3–4, 6–7
    Office of Business Economics, 3–4
    Bureau of International Commerce, 3–4, 19, 34, 37–38
    U.S. Travel Service, 18

Department of Interior:
    Bureau of Land Management, 3–4, 37–38
    Bureau of Mines, 3–4, 34–35, 37–39
    Bureau of Reclamation, 3–4, 6, 31, 34–35, 37–38
    Fish and Wildlife Service, 3–4, 34, 39
    Geological Survey, 3–4
    Office of Territories, 4
    Bureau of Indian Affairs, 4, 34

Department of Justice, 3–4, 37–38

Department of Labor: 3–4
    Bureau of International Labor Affairs, 3–4, 34, 39
    Bureau of Apprenticeship and Training, 3–4, 39
    Bureau of Employment Security, 3–4, 34, 39
    Bureau of Labor Standards, 3–4, 34, 39
    Bureau of Labor Statistics, 3–4, 39
    Women's Bureau, 3–4, 36–37

Post Office Department, 3–4

Department of Treasury:
    Coast Guard, 3–4
    Bureau of Customs, 3–4

Appendix Table 2 (cont.)

Internal Revenue Service, 3–4
Treasury Law Enforcement School, 3–4, 33–34, 37–38
Bureau of Narcotics Training School, 3–4

Atomic Energy Commission, 3–4, 20, 33–34, 37–38

Federal Aviation Agency, 3–4, 6, 34, 36–38

Federal Communications Commission, 3–4, 34, 36–38

General Service Administration:
National Archives, 2–4, 33–34, 37

Housing and Home Finance Agency, 3–4, 36–38

Library of Congress, 3–4, 33–34, 37

Tennessee Valley Authority, 3–4

Smithsonian Institution, 3–4, 31, 33–34, 37

Civil Service Commission, 3–4

Appendix Table 3
THE STATE DEPARTMENT'S EDUCATIONAL AND CULTURAL PROGRAM—1963[1]

Exchange of Persons	$35,199,651
Special Educational and Cultural Projects	5,359,334
Aid to American-sponsored Educational Institutions Abroad	4,603,791
Cultural Presentations	2,822,255
Special Services to Non-grant Students	748,755
UNESCO and Other Multilateral Organization Activities[2]	392,632
Program Services Cost	5,554,350
Administrative Expense Cost	2,035,768
	$56,716,536[3]

[1] Amounts obligated, Fiscal Year 1963.

[2] Does not include the U.S. contribution to UNESCO, handled by a different Bureau of the State Department.

[3] About half of this total is made up of U.S.-owned foreign currencies, obtained from earlier sales of surplus war goods and agricultural products.

Source: Bureau of Educational and Cultural Affairs, U.S. Department of State.

Appendix Table 4
THE STATE DEPARTMENT'S EXCHANGE-OF-PERSONS PROGRAM—1963
Number of Grants by Geographical Areas

	Africa	American Republics	Atlantic Community and Other Western Europe	Eastern Europe	Far East	Near East & South Asia	Total
Students							
Foreign	594	364	927	103	466	600	3,054
United States	2	197	758	75	45	64	1,141
Teachers							
Foreign	22	328	262	8	69	151	840
United States	19	53	306	3	45	111	537
Professors							
Foreign	6	53	372	37	132	84	684
United States	47	130	280	55	166	169	847
Leaders & Specialists							
Foreign	233	320	352	66	292	303	1,566
Specialists—United States	31	57	35	22	67	47	259
Special Projects							
Foreign	113	991	77	4	157	17	1,359
United States	—	—	—	—	—	10	10
Subtotal—Foreign	968	2,056	1,990	218	1,116	1,155	7,503
Subtotal—United States	99	437	1,379	155	323	401	2,794
TOTAL	1,067	2,493	3,369	373	1,439	1,556	10,297

INTERNATIONAL ORGANIZATIONS INVOLVED IN EDUCATIONAL AND CULTURAL AFFAIRS
(To which the United States contributes)

	Support or Assistance to Formal Education
United Nations and Specialized Agencies	
United Nations (proper, including UNTAO)	
UN Children's Fund (UNICEF)	
UN Expanded Program of Technical Assistance (UNTA)	•
UN Relief and Works Agency (UNRWA)	•
UN Special Fund	•
Food and Agriculture Organization (FAO)	•
Intergovernmental Maritime Consultative Organization (IMCO)	
International Civil Aviation Organization (ICAO)	
International Labor Organization (ILO)	
International Telecommunication Union (ITU)	
UN Educational, Scientific, and Cultural Organization (UNESCO)	•
Universal Postal Union (UPU)	
World Health Organization (WHO)	•
World Meteorological Organization (WMO)	
Inter-American Organizations	
Organization of American States (OAS)—Pan American Union	•
OAS Program of Technical Cooperation	
Inter-American Children's Institute	
Inter-American Development Bank (IADB)	•
Inter-American Indian Institute	
Inter-American Institute of Agricultural Sciences	
Pan American Health Organization (PAHO) of WHO	•
Pan American Institute of Geography and History (PAIGH)	
Other Regional Organizations	
North Atlantic Treaty Organization (NATO)	
Asian Productivity Organization (APO)	
Colombo Plan Council for Technical Assistance in S & SE Asia	
Commission for Technical Cooperation in Africa (CCTA)	
Organization for Economic Cooperation and Development (OECD)	
South Pacific Commission	
Southeast Asia Treaty Organization (SEATO)	•
Other International Organizations	
International Atomic Energy Agency (IAEA)	
International Union for the Protection of Industrial Property	
International Bureau of Education	
International Bureau of Weights and Measures	
International Council of Scientific Unions	
International Hydrographic Bureau	
International Bank for Reconstruction and Development (IBRD)	•
International Development Association (IDA)	•
International Monetary Fund	•

Specialized Training	Technical Assistance	Research Support or Projects	Exchange of Persons	Exchange of Technical Documents
●	●	●	●	●
●	●	●	●	
●	●		●	
●				
●	●	●	●	
●	●	●	●	
			●	●
●	●	●	●	●
●	●	●	●	●
●	●		●	●
●	●	●	●	●
	●			●
●	●		●	●
		●	●	
●	●	●	●	●
●	●	●	●	●
●	●		●	●
		●		
●	●	●	●	●
	●			
	●	●		
	●		●	
●	●	●		
		●		
●	●	●	●	●
			●	
		●		●
	●	●		●
		●		●
				●
●			●	
●				

151

Index

Publications of the
COUNCIL ON FOREIGN RELATIONS

FOREIGN AFFAIRS (quarterly), edited by Hamilton Fish Armstrong.
THE UNITED STATES IN WORLD AFFAIRS (annual). Volumes for
1931, 1932 and 1933, by Walter Lippmann and William O.
Scroggs; for 1934–1935, 1936, 1937, 1938, 1939 and 1940, by
Whitney H. Shepardson and William O. Scroggs; for 1945–
1947, 1947–1948 and 1948–1949, by John C. Campbell; for
1949, 1950, 1951, 1952, 1953 and 1954, by Richard P. Stebbins; for 1955, by Hollis W. Barber; for 1956, 1957, 1958,
1959, 1960, 1961, 1962 and 1963, by Richard P. Stebbins.
DOCUMENTS ON AMERICAN FOREIGN RELATIONS (annuals). Volume
for 1952 edited by Clarence W. Baier and Richard P. Steb-
bins; for 1953 and 1954, edited by Peter V. Curl; for 1955,
1956, 1957, 1958 and 1959, edited by Paul E. Zinner; for
1960, 1961, 1962 and 1963 edited by Richard P. Stebbins.
POLITICAL HANDBOOK AND ATLAS OF THE WORLD (annual), edited
by Walter H. Mallory.
FOREIGN AFFAIRS BIBLIOGRAPHY, 1952–1962, by Henry L. Roberts.
JAPAN AND THE UNITED STATES IN WORLD TRADE, by Warren S.
Hunsberger.
THE DOLLAR IN WORLD AFFAIRS, by Henry G. Aubrey.
ON DEALING WITH THE COMMUNIST WORLD, by George F. Kennan.
FOREIGN AID AND FOREIGN POLICY, by Edward S. Mason.
THE SCIENTIFIC REVOLUTION AND WORLD POLITICS, by Caryl P.
Haskins.
AFRICA: A Foreign Affairs Reader, edited by Philip W. Quigg.
THE PHILIPPINES AND THE UNITED STATES: Problems of Partner-
ship, by George E. Taylor.
SOUTHEAST ASIA IN UNITED STATES POLICY, by Russell H. Fifield.
UNESCO: ASSESSMENT AND PROMISE, by George N. Shuster.
THE PEACEFUL ATOM IN FOREIGN POLICY, by Arnold Kramish.
THE ARABS AND THE WORLD: Nasser's Arab Nationalist Policy, by
Charles D. Cremeans.
TOWARD AN ATLANTIC COMMUNITY, by Christian A. Herter.
THE SOVIET UNION, 1922–1962: A Foreign Affairs Reader, edited
by Philip E. Mosely.

Pal Sci.

The Politics of Foreign Aid: American Experience in Southeast Asia, by John D. Montgomery.

Spearheads of Democracy: Labor in the Developing Countries, by George C. Lodge.

Latin America—Diplomacy and Reality, by Adolf A. Berle.

The Organization of American States and the Hemisphere Crisis, by John C. Dreier.

The United Nations: Structure for Peace, by Ernest A. Gross.

The Long Polar Watch: Canada and the Defense of North America, by Melvin Conant.

Arms and Politics in Latin America (Revised Edition), by Edwin Lieuwen.

The Future of Underdeveloped Countries: Political Implications of Economic Development (Revised Edition), by Eugene Staley.

Spain and Defense of the West: Ally and Liability, by Arthur P. Whitaker.

Social Change in Latin America Today: Its Implications for United States Policy, by Richard N. Adams, John P. Gillin, Allan R. Holmberg, Oscar Lewis, Richard W. Patch, and Charles W. Wagley.

Foreign Policy: The Next Phase: The 1960s (Revised Edition), by Thomas K. Finletter.

Defense of the Middle East: Problems of American Policy (Revised Edition), by John C. Campbell.

Communist China and Asia: Challenge to American Policy, by A. Doak Barnett.

France, Troubled Ally: De Gaulle's Heritage and Prospects, by Edgar S. Furniss, Jr.

The Schuman Plan: A Study in Economic Cooperation, 1950–1959, by William Diebold, Jr.

Soviet Economic Aid: The New Aid and Trade Policy in Underdeveloped Countries, by Joseph S. Berliner.

Raw Materials: A Study of American Policy, by Percy W. Bidwell.

Nuclear Weapons and Foreign Policy, by Henry A. Kissinger.

Russia and America: Dangers and Prospects, by Henry L. Roberts.

Foreign Affairs Bibliography, 1942–1952, by Henry L. Roberts.